C000205756

Ben Okri is a poet and novelist and has published many books, including *The Famished Road*, which won the Booker Prize, and *The Age of Magic*. He has also written several poetry collections, including *An African Elegy*, *Mental Fight* and *Wild*. His work has been translated into 27 languages and won numerous international prizes. Born in Nigeria, he lives in London.

Also by Ben Okri

FICTION

Flowers and Shadows
The Landscapes Within
Incidents at the Shrine
Stars of the New Curfew
The Famished Road
Songs of Enchantment
Astonishing the Gods
Infinite Riches
Dangerous Love
In Arcadia
Tales of Freedom
Starbook
The Age of Magic
The Magic Lamp

NON-FICTION

Birds of Heaven
A Way of Being Free
A Time of New Dreams
The Mystery Feast

POETRY

An African Elegy
Mental Fight
Wild

Rise Like Lions

Poetry for the Many

Compiled by Ben Okri

First published in Great Britain in 2017 by Hodder & Stoughton
An Hachette UK company

This paperback edition published in 2018

1

Copyright © Ben Okri 2017

The right of Ben Okri to be identified as the Author of the Work
has been asserted by him in accordance with the Copyright,
Designs and Patents Act 1988.

A CIP catalogue record for this title is available from the British Library

Paperback ISBN 9781473676169
Hardback ISBN 9781473676145
eBook ISBN 9781473676152

Typeset in Minion Pro by
Palimpsest Book Production Ltd, Falkirk, Stirlingshire

Printed and bound in Great Britain by Clays Ltd, Elcograf S.p.A.

Hodder & Stoughton policy is to use papers that are natural, renewable
and recyclable products and made from wood grown in sustainable forests.
The logging and manufacturing processes are expected to conform to the
environmental regulations of the country of origin.

Hodder & Stoughton Ltd
Carmelite House
50 Victoria Embankment
London EC4Y 0DZ

www.hodder.co.uk

To CJ

Contents

3   Protest   75

4   Change   127

5 **Truth   179**

Introduction

Is it a contradiction to speak of political poetry? Some would say that the more of politics there is in a work, the less poetic it is. Is the political antithetical to the poetic? Politics may have to do with power and power is hostile to poetry. This hostility has to do with the fact that poetry is its own power, is its own terrain and universe and at its freest recognises no other. Poetry gets its authority from the voice, from the self, from breath, from the cosmos, from the primal source of freedom itself. Poetry needs no other power for it to be. It needs no other stage to exist except the ear and the eye, the listening heart. Politics is the manipulation of power in the structures of the world. Its territory is the world. This terrestrial monarch called power and this spiritual monarch called poetry are monarchs of realms that fundamentally compete for hegemony. But as our lives are lived in the world, and as our bodies are subjected to the forces of society, it is impossible to escape the emporium of the world. And even poetry, monarch of soul and freedom, finds that on occasion, more often than it would perhaps like, it has to deal with the forms that power indents on our being and our possibility.

For poetry is often roused into being by the ways in which power throttles life and spirit. It is a protest of the soul against the structures and injustices of the world. It is natural that poetry should be roused by injustice, for poetry is the sister of justice, the brother of suffering, and anything that makes the human being cry out touches the core of the human, from which poetry rises. Poetry primarily responds to nature. It is the original breath that is moved by the majesty and the beauty of the world. It is something in us which sings to the sublimity of what appears not to be us but which also appears to be us in unknown ways. Poetry is primarily mystical in that sense, till something obstructs the free flow of its spirit. This is what history does, it is what power does, it is what life does. We ought to be free, but invisible powers fetter us.

We are born into this world 'trailing clouds of glory' and then we find that we are born into poverty or into wealth, born near the gutter or near the palace. These conditions paralyse and strangle the poetic in us, the condition of primal freedom and original beauty. This is why political poetry can be so powerful. It is the original cry of freedom. It is the fundamental cry of man and woman in society. It is profoundly human. Everything after Eden is political. It is the price paid for the expulsion. From paradise to politics is the condition of humanity. From politics back to paradise ought to be the programme of society, a manageable human paradise. The only way there is through poetry. In that sense poetry is the primary programme for the reconstitution of humanity into the possibility of grace, it is by the works of our hands and hearts, of an acceptable society that exalts, respects, unites, and redeems us. No programme of society that intends to bring about a better world is possible without poetry. For poetry is the first estate, the vision of the human from the viewpoint of eternity, the vision of eternity from the aspect of the human.

Poets at their best feel deeply the condition of being human. Poetry is a craft and a difficult one, but its primary power is not in its meters and rhymes, but in the action of its spirit. A skilled poet who does not move us, does not exalt us, does not touch us would really be only a great technician. And it has been the death of poetry to exalt the technique over the spirit, the technique over the awakening. There are poets who are wonderful at what they do, who have the technical mastery, but who leave us cold. They may as well be addressing stones. But incompetence is not acceptable either. Political poetry should not be perceived as the first stop of sentimental poetry, the place where the 'undisciplined squads of emotion' find a convenient home. If the poetry is not of the highest standard it ought not to earn its place as political poetry. As always, it must be good poetry first before it can qualify as political poetry.

Just because someone's heart is in the right place does not justify giving vent to poetry. The best cause in the world does not automatically give validity to poetry. In fact a poetry of causes ought to be suspect, unless it first be an act of poetry, an act of verse-making. Some might even say that the poetry makes the politics.

We are here interested only in those instances where the spirit of poetry has sprung into being through the body of the political. Poetry is always the holy ghost of the combination.

If in this anthology you hear the thunder of politics first we have failed. You ought to first hear the music of poetry. It is the poetry which makes the political element powerful, never the other way round. Just as beauty moves Keats to poetry, so sometimes the sight of a beggar child might move Blake to beauty. The power here is when the poetry is the arrow that sends the shaft of the political into the heart. To be wounded by poetry is more affecting than being bludgeoned by the political. As Keats said, we are always wary when we sense that a work has a design on us. The overtones of the political kill the quiet persuasion of the poetic. For poetry seeks to persuade invisibly, almost as if you were doing it to yourself, with the gentlest hints from the poet. But with political poetry the poet becomes visible and we become suspicious of this used-thought salesman. We hate a conscious pitch. We want to be seduced. The best political poems manage the double feat of seducing you while appearing not to do so, selling you something while somehow keeping the poet absent, in short getting you to sell it to yourself. The mention of selling is repugnant in the realm of poetry. But politics compels its presence. It is the paradox of this twinning which is so fascinating. At best, it is an alchemy.

We live in times in which the media, increasingly in the hands of the powerful, has a compromised hand. A wind of recidivism is sweeping across the world. Everywhere there is felt to be a hunger for a new dimension in public life that can tell us the truth about what is happening. A whole new generation wants truth in ways uncompromised by the secret histories of power ownerships of the medium of information. It is why they take to the Internet and its unregulated freedoms. When information is suspect, when we feel that no one is telling us the truth about the world, it is in such times that the power and freedom of poetry is most bracing. This is a time in which poetry can step forth as a new force in the land.

It is the intention that the poems in this book are on the whole quite short. We wanted poems that could be read in a few moments, but whose impact would be long-lasting. There is a power in brevity.

But there are long poems too. And where it has been deemed necessary to experience the poems in all their force we have not hesitated to include it in its full length. In the end there is no contradiction. There is either the touch or the roar.

Note: Translators are the quiet miracle workers on the universal spirit of poetry. I salute the near impossible work they do. We have included their names in the acknowledgements, but not beside each poem. The translated poem should be experienced purely in the language, as poetry.

1

Ideas

These are seed poems. Here we track the shape of how we become engaged. Poetry itself doesn't have to be engaged to wake us up. All it has to do is awaken in us an unease about the world. Sometimes poems indirectly make you aware that all is not right with the world. Or they make you aware that there is more to the world than we see. Poetry is the primary medium of revealing other realities. The journey of becoming a fully activated citizen begins with a mysterious initiation of experience. For most of our lives we take the world as given. The world that we see is for us the only way the world can be. Our education trains us to be at home with this world. The proverbs and sayings that underlie our grasp of reality tell us not to trouble the surface of the world. The boat is not to be rocked. We are to steadily and gratefully wend our way through life. If there are any evils in the world, they are meant to be. A certain fatalism makes it possible to live without asking questions. Then we come upon certain poems. Quietly they plant new thoughts in our heads.

A single line can shift the tenor of a life. Poetry compresses much into a little: a lifetime of conscious and unconscious contemplation woven into lines of rhythm and beauty. To encounter such poems is to be gently awoken from the dream of life. You might awaken into a landscape of great beauty, in which there is a nameless tomb. You might awaken into a land where some people toil all their lives and others don't. Then you begin to ask questions.

Ideas in poetry are insinuating things. A rhyme can turn the earth of the mind. A single line that lodges in the mind like a burr can quietly overturn a way of seeing the world. Sometimes even an image that seems harmless can undo an entrenched world view. Sometimes a paradox opens up a void in which our certainties are confounded.

3

That we are capable of harbouring opposing ideas at the same time is a curious fact of the human mind. We may abhor the lack of freedom while unthinkingly contributing to conditions that restrict the freedom of others. Poetry can widen those spaces, while doing nothing else but following the logic of its own rhythm, guided by its obscure inspiration.

It is often ideas that get us started on a new road. Ideas alter the vector of our lives. They are the quanta of change. Nothing is possible without a new idea first finding compatibility in our minds. Maybe nothing changes till there is a kind of readiness for change. Maybe only then, when the conditions are right, are we ready for ideas that prepare the ground for change. Sometimes seeds can lie waiting in the earth a long time before conditions are right for them to sprout. But the seeds have to be there first. Seeds are worlds of potentiality. Great ideas often come in small packets. It is perhaps better that way. The smaller they are the more invisibly they infiltrate a system with new light.

But ideas in poetry are protean; for the eternal ambiguity of poetry multiplies its meaning and therefore its ideas. Sometimes we find ideas in poems that didn't seem to have them before. Poems conceal ideas like stamens in buds, like pollen, like leaves in spring.

Jerusalem

William Blake

And did those feet in ancient time
Walk upon England's mountains green?
And was the holy Lamb of God
On England's pleasant pastures seen?

And did the Countenance Divine
Shine forth upon our clouded hills?
And was Jerusalem builded here
Among these dark Satanic Mills?

Bring me my Bow of burning gold!
Bring me my Arrows of desire!
Bring me my Spear! O clouds, unfold!
Bring me my Chariot of fire!

I will not cease from Mental Fight,
Nor shall my sword sleep in my hand,
Till we have built Jerusalem
In England's green and pleasant land.

Pewter

Jack Gilbert

Thrushes flying under the lake. Nightingales singing underground.
Yes, my King. Paris hungry and leisurely just after the war. Yes.
America falling into history. Yes. Those silent winter afternoons
along the Seine when I was always alone. Yes, my King. Rain
everywhere in the forests of Pennsylvania as the king's coach
lumbered and was caught and all stood gathered close
while the black trees went on and on. Ah, my King,
it was the sweet time of our lives: the rain shining on their faces,
the loud sound of rain around. Like the nights we waited,
knowing she was probably warm and moaning under someone else.
That cold mansard looked out over the huge hospital of the poor
and far down on Paris, grey and beautiful under the February rain.
Between that and this. That yes and this yes. Between, my King,
that forgotten girl, forgotten pain, and the consequence.
Those lovely, long-ago night bells that I did not notice grow
more and more apparent in me. Like pewter expanding as it cools.
Yes, like a king halted in the great forest of Pennsylvania.
Like me singing these prison songs to praise the gray,
to praise her, to tell of me, yes, and of you, my King.

The World Is Too Much With Us

William Wordsworth

The world is too much with us; late and soon,
Getting and spending, we lay waste our powers;—
Little we see in Nature that is ours;
We have given our hearts away, a sordid boon!
This Sea that bares her bosom to the moon;
The winds that will be howling at all hours,
And are up-gathered now like sleeping flowers;
For this, for everything, we are out of tune;
It moves us not. Great God! I'd rather be
A Pagan suckled in a creed outworn;
So might I, standing on this pleasant lea,
Have glimpses that would make me less forlorn;
Have sight of Proteus rising from the sea;
Or hear old Triton blow his wreathèd horn.

What Kind of Times are These

Adrienne Rich

There's a place between two stands of trees where the grass grows
     uphill
and the old revolutionary road breaks off into shadows
near a meeting-house abandoned by the persecuted
who disappeared into those shadows.

I've walked there picking mushrooms at the edge of dread, but don't
     be fooled
this isn't a Russian poem, this is not somewhere else but here,
our country moving closer to its own truth and dread,
its own ways of making people disappear.

I won't tell you where the place is, the dark mesh of the woods
meeting the unmarked strip of light—
ghost-ridden crossroads, leafmold paradise:
I know already who wants to buy it, sell it, make it disappear.

And I won't tell you where it is, so why do I tell you
anything? Because you still listen, because in times like these
to have you listen at all, it's necessary
to talk about trees.

Enemy

Langston Hughes

It would be nice
In any case,
To someday meet you
Face to face
Walking down
The road to hell . . .
As I come up
Feeling swell.

Waiting for the Barbarians

C.P. Cavafy

What are we waiting for, assembled in the forum?

   The barbarians are due here today.

Why isn't anything going on in the senate?
Why are the senators sitting there without legislating?

   Because the barbarians are coming today.
   What's the point of senators making laws now?
   Once the barbarians are here, they'll do the legislating.

Why did our emperor get up so early,
and why is he sitting enthroned at the city's main gate,
in state, wearing the crown?

   Because the barbarians are coming today
   and the emperor's waiting to receive their leader.
   He's even got a scroll to give him,
   loaded with titles, with imposing names.

Why have our two consuls and praetors come out today
wearing their embroidered, their scarlet togas?
Why have they put on bracelets with so many amethysts,
rings sparkling with magnificent emeralds?

Why are they carrying elegant canes
beautifully worked in silver and gold?

Because the barbarians are coming today
and things like that dazzle the barbarians.

Why don't our distinguished orators turn up as usual
to make their speeches, say what they have to say?

Because the barbarians are coming today
and they're bored by rhetoric and public speaking.

Why this sudden bewilderment, this confusion?
(How serious people's faces have become.)
Why are the streets and squares emptying so rapidly,
everyone going home lost in thought?

Because night has fallen and the barbarians haven't come.
And some of our men just in from the border say
there are no barbarians any longer.

Now what's going to happen to us without barbarians?
Those people were a kind of solution.

Feasts of Hunger

Arthur Rimbaud

My hunger, Anne, Anne, flee on your donkey.

If I have any taste, it's for hardly anything
but earth and stones.
Dinn! Dinn! Dinn! Dinn!

Let us eat air, rock, coal, iron.
Turn, my hungers.
Feed, hungers, in the meadow of sounds!
Suck the gaudy poison of the convolvuli;
Eat, the stones a poor man breaks,
the old masonry of churches, boulders,
children of floods, loaves lying in the grey valleys!

Hungers, it is bits of black air; the azure trumpeter;
it is my stomach that makes me suffer.
It is unhappiness. Leaves have appeared on earth!
I go looking for the sleepy flesh of fruit.
At the heart of the furrow I pick
Venus' looking-glass and the violet.

My hunger, Anne, Anne, flee on your donkey.

the Cambridge ladies who live in furnished souls

e.e. cummings

the Cambridge ladies who live in furnished souls
are unbeautiful and have comfortable minds
(also, with the church's protestant blessings
daughters, unscented shapeless spirited)
they believe in Christ and Longfellow, both dead,
are invariably interested in so many things—
at the present writing one still finds
delighted fingers knitting for the is it Poles?
perhaps. While permanent faces coyly bandy
scandal of Mrs. N and Professor D
. . . the Cambridge ladies do not care, above
Cambridge if sometimes in its box of
sky lavender and cornerless, the
moon rattles like a fragment of angry candy

In Time of 'The Breaking of Nations'

Thomas Hardy

I
Only a man harrowing clods
In a slow silent walk
With an old horse that stumbles and nods
Half asleep as they stalk.

II
Only thin smoke without flame
From the heaps of couch-grass;
Yet this will go onward the same
Though Dynasties pass.

III
Yonder a maid and her wight
Come whispering by:
War's annals will cloud into night
Ere their story die.

Song of Myself I

Walt Whitman

I
I Celebrate myself, and sing myself,
And what I assume you shall assume,
For every atom belonging to me as good belongs to you.

I loafe and invite my soul,
I lean and loafe at my ease observing a spear of summer grass.

My tongue, every atom of my blood, form'd from this soil, this air,
Born here of parents born here from parents the same, and their
    parents the same,
I, now thirty-seven years old in perfect health begin,
Hoping to cease not till death.

Creeds and schools in abeyance,
Retiring back a while sufficed at what they are, but never forgotten,
I harbor for good or bad, I permit to speak at every hazard,
Nature without check with original energy.

How Beastly the Bourgeois Is

D.H. Lawrence

How beastly the bourgeois is
especially the male of the species—

Presentable, eminently presentable—
shall I make you a present of him?

Isn't he handsome? Isn't he healthy? Isn't he a fine specimen?
Doesn't he look the fresh clean Englishman, outside?
Isn't it God's own image? tramping his thirty miles a day
after partridges, or a little rubber ball?
wouldn't you like to be like that, well off, and quite the
thing?

Oh, but wait!
Let him meet a new emotion, let him be faced with another
man's need,
let him come home to a bit of moral difficulty, let life
face him with a new demand on his understanding
and then watch him go soggy, like a wet meringue.
Watch him turn into a mess, either a fool or a bully.
Just watch the display of him, confronted with a new
demand on his intelligence,
a new life-demand.

How beastly the bourgeois is
especially the male of the species—

Nicely groomed, like a mushroom
standing there so sleek and erect and eyeable—
and like a fungus, living on the remains of a bygone life
sucking his life out of the dead leaves of greater life
than his own.

And even so, he's stale, he's been there too long.
Touch him, and you'll find he's all gone inside
just like an old mushroom, all wormy inside, and hollow
under a smooth skin and an upright appearance.

Full of seething, wormy, hollow feelings
rather nasty—
How beastly the bourgeois is!

Standing in their thousands, these appearances, in damp
England
what a pity they can't all be kicked over
like sickening toadstools, and left to melt back, swiftly
into the soil of England.

The Love Song of J. Alfred Prufrock

T.S. Eliot

> *S'io credesse che mia risposta fosse*
> *A persona che mai tornasse al mondo,*
> *Questa fiamma staria senza piu scosse.*
> *Ma percioche giammai di questo fondo*
> *Non torno vivo alcun, s'i'odo il vero,*
> *Senza tema d'infamia ti rispondo.*

Let us go then, you and I,
When the evening is spread out against the sky
Like a patient etherized upon a table;
Let us go, through certain half-deserted streets,
The muttering retreats
Of restless nights in one-night cheap hotels
And sawdust restaurants with oyster-shells:
Streets that follow like a tedious argument
Of insidious intent
To lead you to an overwhelming question . . .
Oh, do not ask, 'What is it?'
Let us go and make our visit.

In the room the women come and go
Talking of Michelangelo.

The yellow fog that rubs its back upon the window-panes,
The yellow smoke that rubs its muzzle on the window-panes,
Licked its tongue into the corners of the evening,
Lingered upon the pools that stand in drains,
Let fall upon its back the soot that falls from chimneys,

Slipped by the terrace, made a sudden leap,
And seeing that it was a soft October night,
Curled once about the house, and fell asleep.

And indeed there will be time
For the yellow smoke that slides along the street,
Rubbing its back upon the window-panes;
There will be time, there will be time
To prepare a face to meet the faces that you meet;
There will be time to murder and create,
And time for all the works and days of hands
That lift and drop a question on your plate;
Time for you and time for me,
And time yet for a hundred indecisions,
And for a hundred visions and revisions,
Before the taking of a toast and tea.

In the room the women come and go
Talking of Michelangelo.

And indeed there will be time
To wonder, 'Do I dare?' and, 'Do I dare?'
Time to turn back and descend the stair,
With a bald spot in the middle of my hair—
(They will say: 'How his hair is growing thin!')
My morning coat, my collar mounting firmly to the chin,
My necktie rich and modest, but asserted by a simple pin—
(They will say: 'But how his arms and legs are thin!')

Do I dare
Disturb the universe?
In a minute there is time
For decisions and revisions which a minute will reverse.

For I have known them all already, known them all:
Have known the evenings, mornings, afternoons,
I have measured out my life with coffee spoons;
I know the voices dying with a dying fall
Beneath the music from a farther room.
                    So how should I presume?

And I have known the eyes already, known them all—
The eyes that fix you in a formulated phrase,
And when I am formulated, sprawling on a pin,
When I am pinned and wriggling on the wall,
Then how should I begin
To spit out all the butt-ends of my days and ways?
                    And how should I presume?

And I have known the arms already, known them all—
Arms that are braceleted and white and bare
(But in the lamplight, downed with light brown hair!)
Is it perfume from a dress
That makes me so digress?
Arms that lie along a table, or wrap about a shawl.
                    And should I then presume?
                    And how should I begin?

Shall I say, I have gone at dusk through narrow streets
And watched the smoke that rises from the pipes
Of lonely men in shirt-sleeves, leaning out of windows? . . .

I should have been a pair of ragged claws
Scuttling across the floors of silent seas.

And the afternoon, the evening, sleeps so peacefully!
Smoothed by long fingers,
Asleep . . . tired . . . or it malingers,
Stretched on the floor, here beside you and me.
Should I, after tea and cakes and ices,
Have the strength to force the moment to its crisis?
But though I have wept and fasted, wept and prayed,
Though I have seen my head (grown slightly bald) brought in upon
    a platter,
I am no prophet—and here's no great matter;
I have seen the moment of my greatness flicker,
And I have seen the eternal Footman hold my coat, and snicker,
And in short, I was afraid.

And would it have been worth it, after all,
After the cups, the marmalade, the tea,
Among the porcelain, among some talk of you and me,
Would it have been worth while,
To have bitten off the matter with a smile,
To have squeezed the universe into a ball
To roll it towards some overwhelming question,

To say: 'I am Lazarus, come from the dead,
Come back to tell you all, I shall tell you all'—
If one, settling a pillow by her head
   Should say: 'That is not what I meant at all;
   That is not it, at all.'

And would it have been worth it, after all,
Would it have been worth while,
After the sunsets and the dooryards and the sprinkled streets,
After the novels, after the teacups, after the skirts that trail along
   the floor—
And this, and so much more?—
It is impossible to say just what I mean!
But as if a magic lantern threw the nerves in patterns on a screen:
Would it have been worth while
If one, settling a pillow or throwing off a shawl,
And turning toward the window, should say:
   'That is not it at all,
   That is not what I meant, at all.'

No! I am not Prince Hamlet, nor was meant to be;
Am an attendant lord, one that will do
To swell a progress, start a scene or two,
Advise the prince; no doubt, an easy tool,
Deferential, glad to be of use,
Politic, cautious, and meticulous;
Full of high sentence, but a bit obtuse;

At times, indeed, almost ridiculous—
Almost, at times, the Fool.

I grow old . . . I grow old . . .
I shall wear the bottoms of my trousers rolled.

Shall I part my hair behind? Do I dare to eat a peach?
I shall wear white flannel trousers, and walk upon the beach.
I have heard the mermaids singing, each to each.

I do not think that they will sing to me.

I have seen them riding seaward on the waves
Combing the white hair of the waves blown back
When the wind blows the water white and black.
We have lingered in the chambers of the sea
By sea-girls wreathed with seaweed red and brown
Till human voices wake us, and we drown.

Tao Te Ching, Chapter 53

Lao Tzu

If I have a little knowledge
Walking on the great Tao
I fear only to deviate from it
The great Tao is broad and plain
But people like the side paths

The courts are corrupt
The fields are barren
The warehouses are empty

Officials wear fineries
Carry sharp swords
Fill up on drinks and food
Acquire excessive wealth

This is called robbery
It is not the Tao!

The Death of Class

Alexander Pope

I am his Highness' dog at Kew;
Pray tell me, sir, whose dog are you?

England in 1819

Percy Bysshe Shelley

An old, mad, blind, despised, and dying King;
Princes, the dregs of their dull race, who flow
Through public scorn,—mud from a muddy spring;
Rulers who neither see nor feel nor know,
But leechlike to their fainting country cling
Till they drop, blind in blood, without a blow.
A people starved and stabbed in th' untilled field;
An army, whom liberticide and prey
Makes as a two-edged sword to all who wield;
Golden and sanguine laws which tempt and slay;
Religion Christless, Godless—a book sealed;
A Senate, Time's worst statute, unrepealed—
Are graves from which a glorious Phantom may
Burst, to illumine our tempestuous day.

O What Is That Sound

W.H. Auden

O what is that sound which so thrills the ear
　　Down in the valley drumming, drumming?
Only the scarlet soldiers, dear,
　　　　The soldiers coming.

O what is that light I see flashing so clear
　　Over the distance brightly, brightly?
Only the sun on their weapons, dear,
　　　　As they step lightly.

O what are they doing with all that gear
　　What are they doing this morning, this morning?
Only the usual manoeuvres, dear,
　　　　Or perhaps a warning.

O why have they left the road down there
　　Why are they suddenly wheeling, wheeling?
Perhaps a change in the orders, dear,
　　　　Why are you kneeling?

O haven't they stopped for the doctor's care
　　Haven't they reined their horses, their horses?
Why, they are none of them wounded, dear,
　　　　None of these forces.

O is it the parson they want with white hair;
　　Is it the parson, is it, is it?

No, they are passing his gateway, dear,
        Without a visit.

O it must be the farmer who lives so near
    It must be the farmer so cunning, so cunning?
They have passed the farm already, dear,
        And now they are running.

O where are you going? stay with me here!
    Were the vows you swore me deceiving, deceiving?
No, I promised to love you, dear,
        But I must be leaving.

O it's broken the lock and splintered the door,
    O it's the gate where they're turning, turning
Their feet are heavy on the floor
        And their eyes are burning.

The Stare's Nest by My Window

W.B. Yeats

The bees build in the crevices
Of loosening masonry, and there
The mother birds bring grubs and flies.
My wall is loosening; honey-bees,
Come build in the empty house of the stare.

We are closed in, and the key is turned
On our uncertainty; somewhere
A man is killed, or a house burned.
Yet no clear fact to be discerned:
Come build in the empty house of the stare.

A barricade of stone or of wood;
Some fourteen days of civil war:
Last night they trundled down the road
That dead young soldier in his blood:
Come build in the empty house of the stare.

We had fed the heart on fantasies,
The heart's grown brutal from the fare,
More substance in our enmities
Than in our love; O honey-bees,
Come build in the empty house of the stare.

The Times Are Tidy

Sylvia Plath

Unlucky the hero born
In this province of the stuck record
Where the most watchful cooks go jobless
And the mayor's rôtisserie turns
Round of its own accord.

There's no career in the venture
Of riding against the lizard,
Himself withered these latter-days
To leaf-size from lack of action:
History's beaten the hazard.

The last crone got burnt up
More than eight decades back
With the love-hot herb, the talking cat,
But the children are better for it,
The cow milks cream an inch thick.

I hear the oriole's always-grieving voice

Anna Akhmatova

I hear the oriole's always-grieving voice,
And the rich summer's welcome loss I hear
In the sickle's serpentine hiss
Cutting the corn's ear tightly pressed to ear.
And the short skirts of the slim reapers
Fly in the wind like holiday pennants,
The clash of joyful cymbals, and creeping
From under dusty lashes, the long glance.

I don't expect love's tender flatteries,
In premonition of some dark event,
But come, come and see this paradise
Where together we were blessed and innocent.

Come, See Real Flowers

Matsuo Basho

come, see real
flowers
of this painful world

Black Stone on a White Stone

César Vallejo

I will die in Paris with a rainstorm,
on a day I already remember,
I will die in Paris—and I don't shy away—
perhaps on a Thursday, as today is, in autumn.

It will be Thursday, because today, Thursday, as I prose
these lines, I've put on my humeri in a bad mood,
and, today like never before, I've turned back,
with all of my road, to see myself alone.

César Vallejo has died; they kept hitting him,
everyone, even though he does nothing to them,
they gave it to him hard with a club and hard

also with a rope; witnesses are
the Thursday days and the humerus bones,
the solitude, the rain, the roads . . .

2
Vision

Poetry is susceptible to vision. And vision in poetry is both seeing clearly what is there and seeing what will be, what might be, a deeper seeing into the reality of things. But vision here does not always mean the prophetic. In any case each poet has a special meaning they bring to the word vision or the word prophecy. For Yeats vision was a spectral seeing, an occult seeing. For Blake prophecy was not seeing into the future but seeing into the higher states of being or the world. For many poets the word vision is partially synonymous with intensity. And there is a seeing so intense that it reveals unseen aspects of the world. Sometimes a metaphor reveals some underlying condition. We tease it out, we magnify it, and that is enough to reveal the unease in the world, in our lives. That unease is already potent with political implications. Our unease with the world eventually becomes our hidden desire to alter it. Anything that seeks to alter the world is political. Vision is rarely innocent. For it posits an alternative reality to the one we think we know. This is one of the most mysterious functions of poetry. It gives us another reality. In doing so it already begins to put the reality we know in doubt.

We all know that the bible was right when it said that for want of vision a people perish. Vision, more than anything, is what makes leadership. Many nations would be great if they had vision. Many struggles would truly shift the axis of our times if they had vision. There is no shortage of opinion, will, anger, or determination. The greatest lack in our world is vision. We do not have those who can see far enough. We do not have those who can see beyond their temperament, their personal grievances, or even the limitation of their causes or their politics. The far-seers and the clear-seers are rare among us. It is not enough that we have conditions that we want to overcome. It is not enough that we want to change the world. We must have a vision, a worthwhile destination for our fine rage. It ought somehow to begin with us but it ought to end in the wide sea of all of us. This is where poetry transcends politics. Where politics ends, poetry keeps on going on. Politics has its goals, its five-year plans, its election manifestos, but poetry has the steady gaze of an impossible vision that keeps us ever striving to redefine ourselves upwards.

We ought to have a vision that keeps us going beyond the generations. Where others might pitch their tents and say, 'This is enough, we have done well to get here, we need strive no further; this is as much as you can ask of the human capacity for justice and possibility', poetry says, 'This is just the foothill, there are seven mountains ahead.'

We can only ever be measured, not by the distance we have travelled, but by the vision we have. Many would never travel so far if they did not have a vision that was much farther, a vision that cannot be fulfilled by one time, one century, or even a millennium.

At the heart of every people, of every struggle, is the unexpressed vision that animates them, the dream that motivates them, which is to say the poetry that runs in their blood and marrow.

Poems of vision are rare. By its very nature vision places a great strain on poetry. For poetry must speak the invisible through the visible, must touch the transcendent through the contingent, and there are many who prefer the tactile poetry of the *Inferno* to the elusive enchantment of *Paradiso*. Sometimes a vision is a vaporous thing, a thing of clouds and distances. How to make vision concrete and yet intuitive, practical and yet unavoidably wreathed with the mystic rose – these are the challenges of vision in poetry. But it takes a special poet to be receptive to vision, and an even more special poet to find the language and the measure for it. There are poets who are especially gifted with vision. It is almost their special vocation within poetry itself. It separates them from all the others. It requires rare wings to take to the air beyond the clouds. For the most part poetry is a thing of here and now, touching the face, feeling the stone, evoking the waterfall, helping us to be at home in the things and stings of the world.

But we need the poet of vision to compel us to lift up our eyes and to glimpse the light of the rare city beyond the seven mountains. There, that is our destination, there is the home of our feet's journeying, and it shall take us more than our will to get there. It takes the seeing it to make the journey at all. It takes seeing it to make all the struggle and the deaths and the wounds and the sacrifice worthwhile. Then the struggle falls into the right perspective. But without the glimpse, constantly renewed, the struggle might well become meaningless and many will be led astray, and ego and sabotage and secret agendas and old gods might well wreck the nobility of the struggle. And when minor concessions are made many will pitch tents at the roadsides, far from the glimmering heights. And a great dream is surrendered for a pot of false gold.

Poets of vision are the most rigorous of all. It takes great toughness of soul to dream such impractical but impossibly necessary dreams. Poets of vision are also sometimes bearded prophets who walk on with their staff high up into the mountains when their people turn against them and say they are being led too far, that the edge of the river is beautiful enough and the meadows are green, and the children are weary, and decades of wandering and striving should come to an end here in this pleasant valley. Sometimes poets of vision are stoned, or killed, or assassinated, or abandoned, or shunned, or derided. But long after they have gone their visions haunt us. And when the valleys turn cold, and the meadows later yield no food, and the camps fall to dissensions, we perhaps remember once again that our journey is not over, and that our struggles were abandoned when they were in truth only half begun.

Then a new generation, uncontaminated by the compromises of the old, begin again that journey that the poets of vision left behind, left ahead.

But vision too must be parsed, must be re-interpreted with the new times, in the new place. Yet visions never age. They are always ahead of us. Without them we turn to stone.

London

William Blake

I wander through each chartered street,
Near where the chartered Thames does flow,
And mark in every face I meet
Marks of weakness, marks of woe.

In every cry of every man,
In every infant's cry of fear,
In every voice, in every ban,
The mind-forged manacles I hear.

How the chimney-sweeper's cry
Every blackening church appalls,
And the hapless soldier's sigh
Runs in blood down palace walls.

But most through midnight streets I hear
How the youthful harlot's curse
Blasts the new-born infant's tear
And blights with plagues the marriage hearse.

An Irish Airman Foresees his Death

W.B. Yeats

I know that I shall meet my fate
Somewhere among the clouds above;
Those that I fight I do not hate,
Those that I guard I do not love;
My country is Kiltartan Cross,
My countrymen Kiltartan's poor,
No likely end could bring them loss
Or leave them happier than before.
Nor law, nor duty bade me fight,
Nor public man, nor cheering crowds,
A lonely impulse of delight
Drove to this tumult in the clouds;
I balanced all, brought all to mind,
The years to come seemed waste of breath,
A waste of breath the years behind
In balance with this life, this death.

Dover Beach

Matthew Arnold

The sea is calm tonight.
The tide is full, the moon lies fair
Upon the straits; on the French coast the light
Gleams and is gone; the cliffs of England stand,
Glimmering and vast, out in the tranquil bay.
Come to the window, sweet is the night-air!
Only, from the long line of spray
Where the sea meets the moon-blanched land,
Listen! you hear the grating roar
Of pebbles which the waves draw back, and fling,
At their return, up the high strand,
Begin, and cease, and then again begin,
With tremulous cadence slow, and bring
The eternal note of sadness in.

Sophocles long ago
Heard it on the Ægean, and it brought
Into his mind the turbid ebb and flow
Of human misery; we
Find also in the sound a thought,
Hearing it by this distant northern sea.

The Sea of Faith
Was once, too, at the full, and round earth's shore
Lay like the folds of a bright girdle furled.
But now I only hear
Its melancholy, long, withdrawing roar,
Retreating, to the breath

Of the night-wind, down the vast edges drear
And naked shingles of the world.

Ah, love, let us be true
To one another! for the world, which seems
To lie before us like a land of dreams,
So various, so beautiful, so new,
Hath really neither joy, nor love, nor light,
Nor certitude, nor peace, nor help for pain;
And we are here as on a darkling plain
Swept with confused alarms of struggle and flight,
Where ignorant armies clash by night.

Limits XI

Fragments out of the Deluge

Christopher Okigbo

XI
And the gods lie in state
And the gods lie in state
Without the long-drum.

And the gods lie unsung,
Veiled only with mould,
Behind the shrinehouse.

Gods grow out,
Abandoned;
And so do they . . .

Nobel Prize

Boris Pasternak

All is lost, I'm a beast in a pen.
There are people and freedom outside,
But the hunters are already at hand
And I haven't a way to take flight.

The bank of a pond... woods at night
And the trunk of the pine lying bare.
I am trapped and cut off on each side.
Come what comes, I simply don't care.

Am I a murderer, a villain, a creep?
Of what crime do I stand here condemned?
The whole world listens, ready to weep
At my words of my beautiful land.

Even now, at the edge of the tomb,
I believe in the virtuous fate, –
And the spirit of goodness will soon
Overcome all the malice and hate.

Prayer to Masks

Léopold Sédar Senghor

Masks! Masks!
Black mask red mask, you white-and-black masks
Mask of the four points from which the Spirit blows
In silence I salute you!
Nor you the least, the Lion-headed Ancestor
You guard this place forbidden to all laughter of women, to all smiles
    that fade
You distil this air of eternity in which I breathe the air of my
    Fathers.
Masks of unmasked faces, stripped of the marks of illness and the
    lines of age
You who have fashioned this portrait, this my face bent over the
    altar of white paper
In your own image, hear me!
The Africa of the empires is dying, see, the agony of a pitiful
    princess
And Europe too where we are joined by the navel.
Fix your unchanging eyes upon your children, who are given
    orders
Who give away their lives like the poor their last clothes.
Let us report present at the rebirth of the World
Like the yeast which white flour needs.
For who would teach rhythm to a dead world of machines and
    guns?
Who would give the cry of joy to wake the dead and the bereaved
    at dawn?
Say, who would give back the memory of life to the man whose
    hopes are smashed?

They call us men of coffee cotton oil
They call us men of death.
We are the men of the dance, whose feet draw new strength pounding
    the hardened earth.

The Times They Are A-Changin'

Bob Dylan

Come gather 'round people
Wherever you roam
And admit that the waters
Around you have grown
And accept it that soon
You'll be drenched to the bone
If your time to you is worth savin'
Then you better start swimmin' or you'll sink like a stone
For the times they are a-changin'

Come writers and critics
Who prophesise with your pen
And keep your eyes wide
The chance won't come again
And don't speak too soon
For the wheel's still in spin
And there's no tellin' who that it's namin'
For the loser now will be later to win
For the times they are a-changin'

Come senators, congressmen
Please heed the call
Don't stand in the doorway
Don't block up the hall
For he that gets hurt
Will be he who has stalled
There's a battle outside and it is ragin'

It'll soon shake your windows and rattle your walls
For the times they are a-changin'

Come mothers and fathers
Throughout the land
And don't criticise
What you can't understand
Your sons and your daughters
Are beyond your command
Your old road is rapidly agin'
Please get out of the new one if you can't lend your hand
For the times they are a-changin'
The line it is drawn
The curse it is cast
The slow one now
Will later be fast
As the present now
Will later be past
The order is rapidly fadin'
And the first one now will later be last
For the times they are a-changin'

I Hear America Singing

Walt Whitman

I hear America singing, the varied carols I hear,
Those of mechanics, each one singing his as it should be blithe and
   strong,
The carpenter singing his as he measures his plank or beam,
The mason singing his as he makes ready for work, or leaves off
   work,
The boatman singing what belongs to him in his boat, the deckhand
   singing on the steamboat deck,
The shoemaker singing as he sits on his bench, the hatter singing as
   he stands,
The wood-cutter's song, the ploughboy's on his way in the morning,
   or at noon intermission or at sundown,
The delicious singing of the mother, or of the young wife at work,
   or of the girl sewing
   or washing,
Each singing what belongs to him or her and to none else,
The day what belongs to the day—at night the party of young fellows,
   robust, friendly,
Singing with open mouths their strong melodious songs.

Hope is the Thing with Feathers

Emily Dickinson

Hope is the thing with feathers
That perches in the soul,
And sings the tune without the words,
And never stops at all.

And sweetest in the gale is heard;
And sore must be the storm
That could abash the little bird
That kept so many warm.

I've heard it in the chillest land,
And on the strangest sea;
Yet, never, in extremity,
It asked a crumb of me.

Composed upon Westminster Bridge, September 3, 1802

William Wordsworth

Earth has not anything to show more fair:
Dull would he be of soul who could pass by
A sight so touching in its majesty:
This City now doth, like a garment, wear
The beauty of the morning; silent, bare,
Ships, towers, domes, theatres, and temples lie
Open unto the fields, and to the sky;
All bright and glittering in the smokeless air.
Never did sun more beautifully steep
In his first splendour, valley, rock, or hill;
Ne'er saw I, never felt, a calm so deep!
The river glideth at his own sweet will:
Dear God! the very houses seem asleep;
And all that mighty heart is lying still!

On Peace

John Keats

O peace! and dost thou with thy presence bless
The dwellings of this war-surrounded Isle;
Soothing with placid brow our late distress,
Making the triple kingdom brightly smile?
Joyful I hail thy presence; and I hail
The sweet companions that await on thee;
Complete my joy let not my first wish fail,
Let the sweet mountain nymph thy favourite be,
With England's happiness proclaim Europa's Liberty.
O Europe! let not sceptred tyrants see
That thou must shelter in thy former state;
Keep thy chains burst, and boldly say thou art free;
Give thy kings law – leave not uncurbed the great;
So with the horrors past thou'lt win thy happier fate!

To the People of England

Percy Bysshe Shelley

People of England, ye who toil and groan,
Who reap the harvests which are not your own,
Who weave the clothes which your oppressors wear,
And for your own take the inclement air;
Who build warm houses . . .
And are like gods who give them all they have,
And nurse them from the cradle to the grave . . .

The World is a Bundle of Hay

Lord Byron

The world is a bundle of hay,
Mankind are the asses who pull;
Each tugs it a different way,
And the greatest of all is John Bull.

I'm Explaining a Few Things

Pablo Neruda

You are going to ask: and where are the lilacs?
and the poppy-petalled metaphysics?
and the rain repeatedly spattering
its words and drilling them full
of apertures and birds?

I'll tell you all the news.

I lived in a suburb,
a suburb of Madrid, with bells,
and clocks and trees.

From there you could look out
Over Castille's dry face:
a leather ocean.
      My house was called
the house of flowers, because in every cranny
geraniums burst: it was
a good-looking house
with its dogs and children.
      Remember, Raúl?
Eh, Rafael?
      Federico, do you remember
from under the ground
where the light of June drowned flowers in your mouth?
      Brother, my brother!
Everything
loud with big voices, the salt of merchandises,

pile-ups of palpitating bread,
the stalls of my suburb of Argüelles with its statue
Like a drained inkwell in a swirl of hake:
oil flowed into spoons,
a deep baying
of feet and hands swelled in the streets,
metres, litres, the sharp
measure of life,
          stacked-up fish,
the texture of roofs with a cold sun in which
the weather vane falters,
the fine, frenzied ivory of potatoes,
wave on wave of tomatoes rolling down to the sea.

And one morning all that was burning,
one morning the bonfires
leapt out of the earth
devouring human beings—
and from then on fire,
gunpowder from then on,
and from then on blood.
Bandits with planes and Moors,
Bandits with finger-rings and duchesses,
Bandits with black friars spattering blessings
came through the sky to kill children
and the blood of children ran through the streets
without fuss, like children's blood.

Jackals that the jackals would despise,
stones that the dry thistle would bite on and spit out,
vipers that the vipers would abominate!

Face to face with you I have seen the blood
of Spain tower like a tide
to drown you in one wave
of pride and knives!

Treacherous
generals:
see my dead house,
look at broken Spain:

from every house burning metal flows
instead of flowers,
from every socket of Spain
Spain emerges
and from every dead child a rifle with eyes,
and from every crime bullets are born
which will one day find
the bull's eye of your hearts.

And you will ask: why doesn't his poetry
speak of dreams and leaves
and the great volcanoes of his native land?

Come and see the blood in the streets.
Come and see
the blood in the streets.
Come and see the blood
in the streets!

Mercy Mercy Me

Marvin Gaye

Whoa, ah, mercy mercy me
Oh things ain't what they used to be, no no
Where did all the blue skies go?
Poison is the wind that blows from the north and south and east

Whoa mercy, mercy me,
Oh things ain't what they used to be, no no
Oil wasted on the oceans and upon our seas, fish full of mercury

Ah, oh mercy, mercy me
Ah things ain't what they used to be, no no
Radiation under ground and in the sky
Animals and birds who live nearby are dying

Oh mercy, mercy me
Oh things ain't what they used to be
What about this overcrowded land
How much more abuse from man can she stand?

Oh, no no, na, na na, na
My sweet Lord, na, na, na
My Lord, my sweet Lord

The Horses

Edwin Muir

Barely a twelvemonth after
The seven days war that put the world to sleep,
Late in the evening the strange horses came.
By then we had made our covenant with silence,
But in the first few days it was so still
We listened to our breathing and were afraid.
On the second day
The radios failed; we turned the knobs; no answer.
On the third day a warship passed us, heading north,
Dead bodies piled on the deck. On the sixth day
A plane plunged over us into the sea. Thereafter
Nothing. The radios dumb;
And still they stand in corners of our kitchens,
And stand, perhaps, turned on, in a million rooms
All over the world. But now if they should speak,
If on a sudden they should speak again,
If on the stroke of noon a voice should speak,
We would not listen, we would not let it bring
That old bad world that swallowed its children quick
At one great gulp. We would not have it again.
Sometimes we think of the nations lying asleep,
Curled blindly in impenetrable sorrow,
And then the thought confounds us with its strangeness.
The tractors lie about our fields; at evening
They look like dank sea-monsters couched and waiting.
We leave them where they are and let them rust:
'They'll moulder away and be like other loam.'
We make our oxen drag our rusty ploughs,

Long laid aside. We have gone back
Far past our fathers' land.
And then, that evening
Late in the summer the strange horses came.
We heard a distant tapping on the road,
A deepening drumming; it stopped, went on again
And at the corner changed to hollow thunder.
We saw the heads
Like a wild wave charging and were afraid.
We had sold our horses in our fathers' time
To buy new tractors. Now they were strange to us
As fabulous steeds set on an ancient shield.
Or illustrations in a book of knights.
We did not dare go near them. Yet they waited,
Stubborn and shy, as if they had been sent
By an old command to find our whereabouts
And that long-lost archaic companionship.
In the first moment we had never a thought
That they were creatures to be owned and used.
Among them were some half a dozen colts
Dropped in some wilderness of the broken world,
Yet new as if they had come from their own Eden.
Since then they have pulled our ploughs and borne our loads
But that free servitude still can pierce our hearts.
Our life is changed; their coming our beginning.

The Gift Outright

Robert Frost

The land was ours before we were the land's.
She was our land more than a hundred years
Before we were her people. She was ours
In Massachusetts, in Virginia,
But we were England's, still colonials,
Possessing what we still were unpossessed by,
Possessed by what we now no more possessed.
Something we were withholding made us weak
Until we found out that it was ourselves
We were withholding from our land of living,
And forthwith found salvation in surrender.
Such as we were we gave ourselves outright
(The deed of gift was many deeds of war)
To the land vaguely realizing westward,
But still unstoried, artless, unenhanced,
Such as she was, such as she would become.

Dulce et Decorum Est

Wilfred Owen

Bent double, like old beggars under sacks,
Knock-kneed, coughing like hags, we cursed through sludge,
Till on the haunting flares we turned our backs,
And towards our distant rest began to trudge.
Men marched asleep. Many had lost their boots,
But limped on, blood-shod. All went lame; all blind;
Drunk with fatigue; deaf even to the hoots
Of tired, outstripped Five-Nines that dropped behind.

Gas! Gas! Quick, boys!—An ecstasy of fumbling
Fitting the clumsy helmets just in time,
But someone still was yelling out and stumbling
And flound'ring like a man in fire or lime . . .
Dim through the misty panes and thick green light,
As under a green sea, I saw him drowning.

In all my dreams before my helpless sight,
He plunges at me, guttering, choking, drowning.

If in some smothering dreams, you too could pace
Behind the wagon that we flung him in,
And watch the white eyes writhing in his face,
His hanging face, like a devil's sick of sin;
If you could hear, at every jolt, the blood
Come gargling from the froth-corrupted lungs,
Obscene as cancer, bitter as the cud
Of vile, incurable sores on innocent tongues,—

My friend, you would not tell with such high zest
To children ardent for some desperate glory,
The old Lie: *Dulce et decorum est
Pro patria mori.*

Redemption Song

Bob Marley

Old pirates, yes, they rob I
Sold I to the merchant ships
Minutes after they took I
From the bottomless pit
But my hand was made strong
By the hand of the Almighty
We forward in this generation
Triumphantly

Won't you help to sing
These songs of freedom?
'Cause all I ever have
Redemption songs
Redemption songs

Emancipate yourselves from mental slavery
None but ourselves can free our minds
Have no fear for atomic energy
'Cause none of them can stop the time
How long shall they kill our prophets
While we stand aside and look? Ooh
Some say it's just a part of it
We've got to fulfill the book

Won't you help to sing
These songs of freedom?
'Cause all I ever have
Redemption songs

Redemption songs
Redemption songs

Emancipate yourselves from mental slavery
None but ourselves can free our minds
Wo! Have no fear for atomic energy
'Cause none of them-a can-a stop-a the time
How long shall they kill our prophets
While we stand aside and look?
Yes, some say it's just a part of it
We've got to fulfill the book

Won't you have to sing
These songs of freedom?
'Cause all I ever had
Redemption songs
All I ever had
Redemption songs
These songs of freedom
Songs of freedom

Recessional

Rudyard Kipling

God of our fathers, known of old,
Lord of our far-flung battle-line,
Beneath whose awful Hand we hold
Dominion over palm and pine—
Lord God of Hosts, be with us yet,
Lest we forget—lest we forget!

The tumult and the shouting dies;
The Captains and the Kings depart:
Still stands Thine ancient sacrifice,
An humble and a contrite heart.
Lord God of Hosts, be with us yet,
Lest we forget—lest we forget!

Far-called, our navies melt away;
On dune and headland sinks the fire:
Lo, all our pomp of yesterday
Is one with Nineveh and Tyre!
Judge of the Nations, spare us yet,
Lest we forget—lest we forget!

If, drunk with sight of power, we loose
Wild tongues that have not Thee in awe,
Such boastings as the Gentiles use,
Or lesser breeds without the Law—
Lord God of Hosts, be with us yet,
Lest we forget—lest we forget!

For heathen heart that puts her trust
In reeking tube and iron shard,
All valiant dust that builds on dust,
And guarding, calls not Thee to guard,
For frantic boast and foolish word—
Thy mercy on Thy People, Lord!

The Sorrow of Sarajevo

Goran Simić/David Harsent

The Sarajevo wind
leafs through newspapers
that are glued by blood to the street;
I pass with a loaf of bread under my arm.

The river carries the corpse of a woman.
As I run across the bridge
with my canisters of water,
I notice her wristwatch, still in place.

Someone lobs a child's shoe
into the furnace. Family photographs spill
from the back of a garbage truck;
they carry inscriptions:
Love from . . . love from . . . love . . .

There's no way of describing these things,
not really. Each night I wake
and stand by the window to watch my neighbour
who stands by the window to watch the dark.

Silent Hour

Ranier Maria Rilke

Whoever weeps somewhere out in the world
Weeps without cause in the world
Weeps over me.

Whoever laughs somewhere out in the night
Laughs without cause in the night
Laughs at me.

Whoever wanders somewhere in the world
Wanders in vain in the world
Wanders to me.

Whoever dies somewhere in the world
Dies without cause in the world
Looks at me.

The Black Heralds

César Vallejo

There are in life such hard blows . . . I don't know!
Blows seemingly from God's wrath; as if before them
the undertow of all our sufferings
is embedded in our souls . . . I don't know!

There are few; but are . . . opening dark furrows
in the fiercest of faces and the strongest of loins,
They are perhaps the colts of barbaric Attilas
or the dark heralds Death sends us.

They are the deep falls of the Christ of the soul,
of some adorable one that Destiny Blasphemes.
Those bloody blows are the crepitation
of some bread getting burned on us by the oven's door

And the man . . . poor . . . poor!
He turns his eyes around, like
when patting calls us upon our shoulder;
he turns his crazed maddened eyes,
and all of life's experiences become stagnant, like a puddle of guilt,
    in a daze.

There are such hard blows in life. I don't know.

To the Students of the Workers' and Peasants' Faculty

Bertolt Brecht

So there you sit. And how much blood was shed
That you might sit there. Do such stories bore you?
Well, don't forget that others sat before you
who later sat on people. Keep your head!
Your science will be valueless, you'll find
And learning will be sterile, if inviting
Unless you pledge your intellect to fighting
Against all enemies of all mankind.
Never forget that men like you got hurt
That you might sit here, not the other lot.
And now don't shut your eyes, and don't desert
But learn to learn, and try to learn for what.

3
Protest

Sometimes poetry, roused by something intolerable in society, awoken by some injustice, rises to the condition of protest. Sometimes the poet is so choked by the foulness of the world, or some unacceptable condition of society, that they abandon briefly the woods and flowers and love ditties to sound a powerful note. It is felt by some that poetry should never be used for something so indelicate as protest, something so clumsy as politics. But the greater the sensitivities of the poet to the plight of his or her fellow human beings the more it becomes impossible to be silent about that which is crushing them. It may well be that the poetry of protest is relatively recent in the history of poetry for a number of reasons. Chief among them is that traditionally in the West the poet has tended to belong to the upper or at least the upper middle classes. They tended to belong to the establishment. The other reason is the very tradition of poetry itself. Its long and distinguished history has seen poetry often at the service of the mythology of state, often at the service of power. Poets were the bards and the recorders. They were often in the employment of kings. Poetry itself was early on allied to mythology. In its lyric phase poetry address the themes of nature, of love, of death, of the transience of life. It was only with the rise of modern states, when they became increasingly divorced from the establishment, that the poet saw the injustices of society as a worthwhile subject for verse.

To protest is to say no. It is to find certain things unacceptable. It is to say that fundamentally you believe that something can be changed, that the world can be altered. When the poet chooses to protest they use the finest instrument they have and they sing with delicacy and with power of the ills of society. When Beethoven was asked about the nature of music, he gave the example of martial music, which makes you want to march. Music, he contended, takes you over. It is a force that works in your blood. The poet must have discovered that poetry affects us spiritually, intellectually, but also physically. And when the poet leaves off celebrating nature or writing love songs, and turns their eye towards the state of the world, a new power is born in their songs. The note of protest sounds strongly in the poetry of Byron, of Shelley, of Blake, and of Yeats. Protest has connections with the Romantic movement. It may have been that inherent in Romanticism is the belief that the world can be changed, and that poetry, along with politics, is one of the high powers in the world. It was Shelley who famously declared that 'poets are the unacknowledged legislators of the world'. The meaning of that phrase has been richly and inconclusively debated. But its intent cannot be in doubt: that poetry helps make the invisible laws of the world.

It is finally a matter of responsibility. Those who see something unacceptable and choose to keep quiet unintentionally allow the unacceptable to be uncontested and therefore legitimate. There are poets who believe that poetry should not get mixed up with the sordid stuff of politics and society. But this is to regard the poet as removed from society, unaffected by it, or somehow above it. But poetry is language and language is part of the fabric of power, of the laws, of the making and the unmaking of society. By the very nature of language the poet, whether they choose to accept it or not, is part of the order of things. There is a sense in which it is impossible not to write about one's times. Even reticence about the central defining issues of the day speaks in that reticence, speaks in the negative space of metaphor, speaks in the very images used. The poet is saturated in their times due to their unconscious absorbent sensibility.

But the poetry of protest is born when the poet looks at the world and says no. They say no with all the beauty and truth with which they said yes to daffodils and tempests. They say no with high craft and cunning strategies. The best poets never let protest depress their verse. In many cases protest gives a new, heightened life to their poetry. At last they are grappling, in an eternal way, with the issues burning up their generation. Whether it is war, poverty, injustice, gulags, slums, racism, poets have found new ways to register the vote of their sensibility in the democracy of expression.

Sometimes the poet writes poems of protest just to register the unacceptable face of society. Sometimes naming an evil is enough. Then the rest of us can see it, and those of us who know how to magnify voices can then try to change the laws and alter the conditions in the world. The power of naming is the power of making visible.

The poets chosen here wrote some of their best poems in the spirit of protest. Sometimes the protest is direct. But often it is indirect, and has to be deduced from the rhythm, from the images and metaphors, and from the tone. The best protest poems can be rousing, or they can quietly shift your thoughts and feelings about the world. They always show, by indirection, that the world's visage is not fixed. Like Okigbo, like Akhmatova, like Yeats, they say no in thunder.

It is when we begin to protest that we begin to rise to our human potential to shake the foundations of the world, so that justice may prevail. Poetry is most human when it allies itself with justice.

Roll of Thunder, Hear my Cry

African-American Spiritual

Roll of thunder
Hear my cry
Over the water
Bye and bye
Ole man comin'
Down the line
Whip in hand to
Beat me down
But I ain't
Gonna let him
Turn me around.

The Poor Man Dreams

Arthur Rimbaud

Perhaps an Evening awaits me
When I shall drink in peace
In some old Town,
And die the happier:
Since I am patient!

If my pain submits,
If I ever have any gold,
Shall I choose the North
Or the Country of Vines? . . .
—Oh! It is shameful to dream

Since it is pure loss!
And if I become once more
The old traveller,
Never can the green inn
Be open to me again.

And you, my friends who have been called away

Anna Akhmatova

And you, my friends who have been called away,
I have been spared to mourn for you and weep,
Not as a frozen willow over your memory,
But to cry to the world the names of those who sleep.
What names are those!
I slam shut the calendar,
Down on your knees, all!
Blood of my heart,
The people of Leningrad march out in even rows,
The living, the dead: fame can't tell them apart.

Poet grieving over shivering monkeys

Matsuo Basho

Poet grieving over shivering
monkeys, what of this child
cast out in autumn wind?

A Far Cry from Africa

Derek Walcott

A wind is ruffling the tawny pelt
Of Africa. Kikuyu, quick as flies,
Batten upon the bloodstreams of the veldt.
Corpses are scattered through a paradise.
Only the worm, colonel of carrion, cries:
'Waste no compassion on these separate dead!'
Statistics justify and scholars seize
The salients of colonial policy.
What is that to the white child hacked in bed?
To savages, expendable as Jews?

Threshed out by beaters, the long rushes break
In a white dust of ibises whose cries
Have wheeled since civilisation's dawn
From the parched river or beast-teeming plain.
The violence of beast on beast is read
As natural law, but upright man
Seeks his divinity by inflicting pain.
Delirious as these worried beasts, his wars
Dance to the tightened carcass of a drum,
While he calls courage still that native dread
Of the white peace contracted by the dead.

Again brutish necessity wipes its hands
Upon the napkin of a dirty cause, again
A waste of our compassion, as with Spain,
The gorilla wrestles with the superman.
I who am poisoned with the blood of both,

Where shall I turn, divided to the vein?
I who have cursed
The drunken officer of British rule, how choose
Between this Africa and the English tongue I love?
Betray them both, or give back what they give?
How can I face such slaughter and be cool?
How can I turn from Africa and live?

The Poor of the Earth Hide Together

Job 24:1-7

1 Why, seeing times are not hidden
   from the Almighty,
   do they that know him
   not see his days?

2 Some remove the landmarks;
   they violently take away flocks,
   and feed thereof.

3 They drive away the ass
   of the fatherless,
   they take the widow's ox
   for a pledge.

4 They turn the needy
   out of the way:
   the poor of the earth
   hide themselves together.

5 Behold, as wild asses in the desert,
   go they forth to their work;
   rising betimes for a prey:
   the wilderness
   yieldeth food for them
   and for their children.

6 They reap every one
   his corn in the field:

and they gather the vintage
of the wicked.

7 They cause the naked
  to lodge without clothing,
  that they have no covering
  in the cold.

The Incandescence of the Wind

Ben Okri

The incandescence of the wind
bothers me
in this vineyard.
Is there a searing clarity
about the noises
rising daily
from this riverbed we call our own?

The yam-tubers bleed our sorrows.
Crows in the fields
scream of despair.
Machetes pollute our food
with rust.
The masters conduct their
plunderings
with quiet murders:
The victims perform maypole dances
around the village shrines.

There is a cold fire in the air.
I hear it
consume the groins
of heroes
and shrivel the guts
of martyrs.
The name of the fire
is printed on grave stones:

names squeezed from tubers of life
and collective cowardice.

At night mothers scream
of children lost in the city fires
of children lost in neon signs
and cellars of madness.
I hear noises from the streets:
men are lost in files
or have wandered
into the fractured severity
of military gun-shots
have become a generation
drenched in petrol
camp-fired
and barbecued
in the fevers
of elections
riots
coups.

The incandescence in the air
burns inward.
Is there a name for this fear?
Is there a fearful country
in these fields
where such realities are
manufactured whole?

I heard a secret
in the burning iron of the mornings.
Animals
have delivered eggs of blood.
Women
have discovered the secret
of an inviolable flesh-haze.
There are multiple deaths
in the riverbeds
and junkyards
polluting our world
with an irascible sense
of failure.
Shall we join them
or shall we celebrate
the vision of empty offices
the short-sightedness of power.

Break the bread
of initiation into
revolt:
We shall celebrate with our
emaciated chests.
We shall clench and raise our fists
in the wonder of incandescence.

I hear a light
bursting up through

the bright blue roots
and the yellow skeletons.
We have breathed
our self-love in those bones.
We have breathed
incantations
at those worms
that ravage our serenity.

The graveyards heave.
The riverbeds sigh.
And I wake surprised:
   – the incandescence has become
  our own
   – the skeletons have reclaimed
  the lands
   – a new spirit breathing phosphorous
  has grown
  into the blue roots of the times.

August 1982

A dog's obeyed in office

William Shakespeare

KING LEAR

And the creature run from the cur? There thou mightst behold the
   great image of authority: a dog's obeyed in office.
Thou rascal beadle, hold thy bloody hand!
Why dost thou lash that whore? Strip thine own back.
Thou hotly lusts to use her in that kind
For which thou whip'st her. The usurer hangs the cozener.
Through tattered clothes small vices do appear;
Robes and furred gowns hide all. Plate sin with gold,
And the strong lance of justice hurtless breaks.
Arm it in rags, a pigmy's straw does pierce it.
None does offend—none, I say, none. I'll able 'em.
Take that of me, my friend, who have the power
To seal th' accuser's lips. Get thee glass eyes,
And, like a scurvy politician, seem
To see the things thou dost not. Now, now, now, now,
Pull off my boots. Harder, harder. So.

University of Hunger

Martin Carter

is the university of hunger the wide waste.
is the pilgrimage of man the long march.
The print of hunger wanders in the land.
The green tree bends above the long forgotten.
The plains of life rise up and fall in spasms.
The huts of men are fused in misery.

They come treading in the hoofmarks of the mule
passing the ancient bridge
the grave of pride
the sudden flight
the terror and the time.

They come from the distant village of the flood
passing from middle air to middle earth
in the common hours of nakedness.

Twin bars of hunger mark their metal brows
twin seasons mock them
parching drought and flood.

is the dark ones
the half sunken in the land.
is they who had no voice in the emptiness
in the unbelievable
in the shadowless.

They come treading on the mud floor of the year
mingling with dark heavy waters
and the sea sound of the eyeless flitting bat.
O long is the march of men and long is the life
and wide is the span.

is the air dust and the long distance of memory
is the hour of rain when sleepless toads are silent
is broken chimneys smokeless in the wind
is brown trash huts and jagged mounds of iron

They come in long lines toward the broad city
is the golden moon like a big coin in the sky
is the floor of bone beneath the floor of flesh
is the beak of sickness breaking on the stone
O long is the march of men, and long is the life
and wide is the span
O cold is the cruel wind blowing.
O cold is the hoe in the ground.

They come like sea birds
flapping in the wake of a boat
is the torture of sunset in purple bandages
is the powder of the fire spread like dust in the twilight
is the water melodies of white foam on wrinkled sand.

The long streets of night move up and down
baring the thighs of a woman.

and the cavern of generation.
The beating drum returns and dies away.
The bearded men fall down and go to sleep.
The cocks of dawn stand up and crow like bugles.

is they who rose early in the morning
watching the moon die in the dawn.
is they who heard the shell blow and the iron clang.
is they who had no voice in the emptiness
in the unbelievable
in the shadowless.
O long is the march of men and long is the life
and wide is the span.

Anthem for Doomed Youth

Wilfred Owen

What passing-bells for these who die as cattle?
Only the monstrous anger of the guns.
Only the stuttering rifles' rapid rattle
Can patter out their hasty orisons.
No mockeries now for them; no prayers nor bells;
Nor any voice of mourning save the choirs,—
The shrill, demented choirs of wailing shells;
And bugles calling for them from sad shires.

What candles may be held to speed them all?
Not in the hands of boys, but in their eyes
Shall shine the holy glimmers of goodbyes.
The pallor of girls' brows shall be their pall;
Their flowers the tenderness of patient minds,
And each slow dusk a drawing-down of blinds.

Nagasaki Days

for Michael Brownstein and Dick Gallup

Allen Ginsberg

I – A Pleasant Afternoon

One day 3 poets and 60 ears sat under a green-striped Chautauqua
tent in Aurora
listening to Black spirituals, tapping their feet, appreciating
words singing by in mountain winds
on a pleasant sunny day of rest—the wild wind blew thru
blue Heavens
filled with fluffy clouds stretched from Central City to Rocky
Flats, Plutonium sizzled in its secret bed,
hot dogs sizzled in the Lion's Club lunchwagon microwave
mouth, orangeade bubbled over in waxen cups
Traffic moved along Colefax, meditators silent in the Diamond
Castle shrine-room at Boulder followed the breath going
out of their nostrils,
Nobody could remember anything, spirits flew out of mouths
& noses, out of the sky, across Colorado plains & the
tent flapped happily open spacious & didn't fall down.

June 18, 1978
II – Peace Protest
Cumulus clouds float across blue sky
over the white-walled Rockwell Corporation factory
—am I going to stop that?

*

Rocky Mountains rising behind us
Denver shining in morning light
—Led away from the crowd by police and photographers

*

Middle-aged Ginsberg and Ellsberg taken down the road
to the grey-haired Sheriff's van—
But what about Einstein? What about Einstein? Hey, Einstein
Come back!

III – *Golden Courthouse*
Waiting for the Judge, breathing silent
Prisoners, witnesses, Police—
the stenographer yawns into her palms.

August 9, 1978
IV – *Everybody's Fantasy*
I walked outside & the bomb'd
dropped lots of plutonium
all over the Lower East Side
There weren't any buildings left just
iron skeletons
groceries burned, potholes open to
stinking sewer waters

There were people starving and crawling
across the desert
the Martian UFOs with blue
Light destroyer rays

passed over and dried up all the
waters

Charred Amazon palm trees for
hundreds of miles on both sides
of the river

August 10, 1978
V - Waiting Room at the Rocky Flats Plutonium Plant
'Give us the weapons we need to protect ourselves!'
the bareheaded guard lifts his flyswatter above the desk —whap!

*

A green-letter'd shield on the pressboard wall!
'Life is fragile. Handle with care' —
My Goodness! here's where they make the nuclear bomb
triggers.

August 17, 1978
VI - Numbers in Red Notebook
2,000,000 killed in Vietnam
13,000,000 refugees in Indochina 1972
200,000,000 years for the Galaxy to revolve on its core
24,000 the Babylonian Great Year
24,000 half life of plutonium
2,000 the most I ever got for a poetry reading
80,000 dolphins killed in the dragnet
4,000,000,000 years earth been born
Summer 1978

On a Political Prisoner

W.B. Yeats

She that but little patience knew,
From childhood on, had now so much
A grey gull lost its fear and flew
Down to her cell and there alit,
And there endured her fingers' touch
And from her fingers ate its bit.

Did she in touching that lone wing
Recall the years before her mind
Became a bitter, an abstract thing,
Her thought some popular enmity:
Blind and leader of the blind
Drinking the foul ditch where they lie?

When long ago I saw her ride
Under Ben Bulben to the meet,
The beauty of her country-side
With all youth's lonely wildness stirred,
She seemed to have grown clean and sweet
Like any rock-bred, sea-borne bird:

Sea-borne, or balanced on the air
When first it sprang out of the nest
Upon some lofty rock to stare
Upon the cloudy canopy,
While under its storm-beaten breast
Cried out the hollows of the sea.

Elegy for Alto

(With drum accompaniment)

Christopher Okigbo

AND THE HORN may now paw the air howling goodbye . . .
For the Eagles are now in sight:
Shadows in the horizon—
THE ROBBERS are here in black sudden steps of showers, of
caterpillars—
THE EAGLES have come again,
The eagles rain down on us—
POLITICIANS are back in giant hidden steps of howitzers, of
detonators—
THE EAGLES descend on us,
Bayonets and cannons—
THE ROBBERS descend on us to strip us of our laughter, of our
    thunder—
THE EAGLES have chosen their game,
Taken our concubines—
POLITICIANS are here in this iron dance of mortars, of generators—

THE EAGLES are suddenly there,
New stars of iron dawn;
O let the horn paw the air howling goodbye . . .
O mother mother Earth, unbind me; let this be
my last testament; let this be
The ram's hidden wish to the sword the sword's
secret prayer to the scabbard—

THE ROBBERS are back in black hidden steps of detonators—
FOR BEYOND the blare of sirened afternoons, beyond

the motorcades;
Beyond the voices and days, the echoing highways; beyond the
    latescence
Of our dissonant airs; through our curtained eyeballs,
through our shuttered sleep,
Onto our forgotten selves, onto our broken images;
beyond the barricades
Commandments and edicts, beyond the iron tables,
beyond the elephant's
Legendary patience, beyond his inviolable bronze
bust; beyond our crumbling towers—
BEYOND the iron path careering along the same beaten track—
THE GLIMPSE of a dream lies smouldering in a cave,
together with the mortally wounded birds.
Earth, unbind me; let me be the prodigal; let this be
the ram's ultimate prayer to the tether . . .

AN OLD STAR departs, leaves us here on the shore
Gazing heavenward for a new star approaching;
The new star appears, foreshadows its going
Before a going and coming that goes on forever . . .

Listen Comrades

David Diop

Listen comrades of incendiary centuries
To the flaming black outcry from Africa to the Americas
They have killed Mamba
As they did the seven at Martinsville
As they did the Malagasy in the livid crackle of prisons
In his look comrades there was
The warm fidelity of an untormented heart
And beyond the pain
Beyond the wounds on his flailed body
His smile kept the bright colors of a bouquet of hope
It's true they've killed him white-haired Mamba
Who ten times poured us milk and light
On my dreams I feel his mouth
And the calm throb of his breast
And my memory hurts
Like the plant torn from the maternal womb
But no
Now higher than my grief
Purer than the morning when the wild beast woke
Bursts the cry of a hundred peoples smashing dens
And the blood of my years of exile
Blood they thought was running dry in the coffin of words
Regains the fervor that pierces fogs
Listen comrades of incendiary centuries
To the flaming black outcry from Africa to the Americas
It is the sign of dawn
The fraternal sign that will come and feed the dreams of men.

A Hard Rain's A-Gonna Fall

Bob Dylan

Oh, where have you been, my blue-eyed son?
Oh, where have you been, my darling young one?
I've stumbled on the side of twelve misty mountains
I've walked and I've crawled on six crooked highways
I've stepped in the middle of seven sad forests
I've been out in front of a dozen dead oceans
I've been ten thousand miles in the mouth of a graveyard
And it's a hard, and it's a hard, it's a hard, and it's a hard
And it's a hard rain's a-gonna fall

Oh, what did you see, my blue-eyed son?
Oh, what did you see, my darling young one?
I saw a newborn baby with wild wolves all around it
I saw a highway of diamonds with nobody on it
I saw a black branch with blood that kept drippin'
I saw a room full of men with their hammers a-bleedin'
I saw a white ladder all covered with water
I saw ten thousand talkers whose tongues were all broken
I saw guns and sharp swords in the hands of young children
And it's a hard, and it's a hard, it's a hard, it's a hard
And it's a hard rain's a-gonna fall

And what did you hear, my blue-eyed son?
And what did you hear, my darling young one?
I heard the sound of a thunder, it roared out a warnin'
Heard the roar of a wave that could drown the whole world
Heard one hundred drummers whose hands were a-blazin'
Heard ten thousand whisperin' and nobody listenin'

Heard one person starve, I heard many people laughin'
Heard the song of a poet who died in the gutter
Heard the sound of a clown who cried in the alley
And it's a hard, and it's a hard, it's a hard, it's a hard
And it's a hard rain's a-gonna fall

Oh, who did you meet, my blue-eyed son?
Who did you meet, my darling young one?
I met a young child beside a dead pony
I met a white man who walked a black dog
I met a young woman whose body was burning
I met a young girl, she gave me a rainbow
I met one man who was wounded in love
I met another man who was wounded with hatred
And it's a hard, it's a hard, it's a hard, it's a hard
It's a hard rain's a-gonna fall

Oh, what'll you do now, my blue-eyed son?
Oh, what'll you do now, my darling young one?
I'm a-goin' back out 'fore the rain starts a-fallin'
I'll walk to the depths of the deepest black forest
Where the people are many and their hands are all empty
Where the pellets of poison are flooding their waters
Where the home in the valley meets the damp dirty prison
Where the executioner's face is always well hidden
Where hunger is ugly, where souls are forgotten
Where black is the colour, where none is the number
And I'll tell it and think it and speak it and breathe it

And reflect it from the mountain so all souls can see it
Then I'll stand on the ocean until I start sinkin'
But I'll know my song well before I start singin'
And it's a hard, it's a hard, it's a hard, it's a hard
It's a hard rain's a-gonna fall

The Prisoner of Chillon (extract)

Lord Byron

My hair is grey, but not with years,
Nor grew it white
In a single night,
As men's have grown from sudden fears;
My limbs are bow'd, though not with toil,
But rusted with a vile repose,
For they have been a dungeon's spoil,
And mine has been the fate of those
To whom the goodly earth and air
Are bann'd, and barr'd—forbidden fare;
But this was for my father's faith
I suffer'd chains and courted death;
That father perish'd at the stake
For tenets he would not forsake;
And for the same his lineal race
In darkness found a dwelling place.
We were seven—who now are one,
Six in youth, and one in age,
Finish'd as they had begun,
Proud of Persecution's rage;
One in fire, and two in field,
Their belief with blood have seal'd,
Dying as their father died,
For the God their foes denied;
Three were in a dungeon cast,
Of whom this wreck is left the last.

There are seven pillars of Gothic mould,
In Chillon's dungeons deep and old,
There are seven columns, massy and grey,
Dim with a dull imprison'd ray,
A sunbeam which hath lost its way,
And through the crevice and the cleft
Of the thick wall is fallen and left;
Creeping o'er the floor so damp,
Like a marsh's meteor lamp.
And in each pillar there is a ring,
And in each ring there is a chain;
That iron is a cankering thing,
For in these limbs its teeth remain,
With marks that will not wear away,
Till I have done with this new day,
Which now is painful to these eyes,
Which have not seen the sun so rise
For years—I cannot count them o'er,
I lost their long and heavy score
When my last brother droop'd and died,
And I lay living by his side.

They chain'd us each to a column stone,
And we were three—yet, each alone;
We could not move a single pace,
We could not see each other's face,
But with that pale and livid light
That made us strangers in our sight:

And thus together—yet apart,
Fetter'd in hand, but join'd in heart,
'Twas still some solace, in the dearth
Of the pure elements of earth,
To hearken to each other's speech,
And each turn comforter to each
With some new hope, or legend old,
Or song heroically bold;
But even these at length grew cold.
Our voices took a dreary tone,
An echo of the dungeon stone,
A grating sound, not full and free,
As they of yore were wont to be;
It might be fancy—but to me
They never sounded like our own.

***

It might be months, or years, or days—
I kept no count, I took no note—
I had no hope my eyes to raise,
And clear them of their dreary mote.
At last men came to set me free;
I ask'd not why, and reck'd not where;
It was at length the same to me,
Fetter'd or fetterless to be,
I learn'd to love despair.
And thus when they appear'd at last,
And all my bonds aside were cast,

These heavy walls to me had grown
A hermitage—and all my own!
And half I felt as they were come
To tear me from a second home:
With spiders I had friendship made
And watch'd them in their sullen trade,
Had seen the mice by moonlight play,
And why should I feel less than they?
We were all inmates of one place,
And I, the monarch of each race,
Had power to kill—yet, strange to tell!
In quiet we had learn'd to dwell;
My very chains and I grew friends,
So much a long communion tends
To make us what we are:—even I
Regain'd my freedom with a sigh.

The Tower of Famine

Percy Bysshe Shelley

Amid the desolation of a city,
Which was the cradle, and is now the grave
Of an extinguished people,—so that Pity

Weeps o'er the shipwrecks of Oblivion's wave,
There stands the Tower of Famine. It is built
Upon some prison-homes, whose dwellers rave

For bread, and gold, and blood: Pain, linked to Guilt,
Agitates the light flame of their hours,
Until its vital oil is spent or spilt.

There stands the pile, a tower amid the towers
And sacred domes; each marble-ribbed roof,
The brazen-gated temples, and the bowers

Of solitary wealth,—the tempest-proof
Pavilions of the dark Italian air,—
Are by its presence dimmed—they stand aloof,

And are withdrawn—so that the world is bare;
As if a spectre wrapped in shapeless terror
Amid a company of ladies fair

Should glide and glow, till it became a mirror
Of all their beauty, and their hair and hue,
The life of their sweet eyes, with all its error,
Should be absorbed, till they to marble grew.

Written on the Day that
Mr Leigh Hunt Left Prison

John Keats

What though, for showing truth to flatter'd state,
Kind Hunt was shut in prison, yet has he,
In his immortal spirit, been as free
As the sky-searching lark, and as elate.
Minion of grandeur! think you he did wait?
Think you he nought but prison walls did see,
Till, so unwilling, thou unturn'dst the key?
Ah, no! far happier, nobler was his fate!
In Spenser's halls he stray'd, and bowers fair,
Culling enchanted flowers; and he flew
With daring Milton through the fields of air:
To regions of his own his genius true
Took happy flights. Who shall his fame impair
When thou art dead, and all thy wretched crew?

To Toussaint L'Ouverture

William Wordsworth

Toussaint, the most unhappy man of men!
Whether the whistling rustic tend his plough
Within thy hearing, or thy head be now
Pillowed in some deep dungeon's earless den;–
O miserable Chieftain! where and when
Wilt thou find patience! Yet die not; do thou
Wear rather in thy bonds a cheerful brow:
Though fallen Thyself, never to rise again,
Live, and take comfort. Thou hast left behind
Powers that will work for thee; air, earth, and skies;
There's not a breathing of the common wind
That will forget thee; thou hast great allies;
Thy friends are exultations, agonies,
And love, and man's unconquerable mind.

Sonnet XVI: Cromwell, Our Chief of Men

To the Lord General Cromwell, May 1652,
On the proposals of certain ministers at the
Committee for Propagation of the Gospel

John Milton

Cromwell, our chief of men, who through a cloud
   Not of war only, but detractions rude,
   Guided by faith and matchless fortitude,
   To peace and truth thy glorious way hast plough'd,
And on the neck of crowned Fortune proud
   Hast rear'd God's trophies, and his work pursu'd,
   While Darwen stream with blood of Scots imbru'd,
   And Dunbar field, resounds thy praises loud,
And Worcester's laureate wreath; yet much remains
   To conquer still: peace hath her victories
   No less renown'd than war. New foes arise
Threat'ning to bind our souls with secular chains:
   Help us to save free Conscience from the paw
   Of hireling wolves whose gospel is their maw.

To a Foil'd European Revolutionaire

Walt Whitman

Courage yet, my brother or my sister!
Keep on—Liberty is to be subserv'd whatever occurs;
That is nothing that is quell'd by one or two failures, or any number
   of failures,
Or by the indifference or ingratitude of the people, or by any unfaith-
   fulness,
Or the show of the tushes of power, soldiers, cannon, penal statutes.

What we believe in waits latent forever through all the continents,
Invites no one, promises nothing, sits in calmness and light, is posi-
   tive and composed, knows no discouragement,
Waiting patiently, waiting its time.

(Not songs of loyalty alone are these,
But songs of insurrection also,
For I am the sworn poet of every dauntless rebel the world over,
And he going with me leaves peace and routine behind him,
And stakes his life to be lost at any moment.)

The battle rages with many a loud alarm and frequent advance and
   retreat,
The infidel triumphs, or supposes he triumphs,
The prison, scaffold, garroté, handcuffs, iron necklace and leadballs
   do their work,
The named and unnamed heroes pass to other spheres,
The great speakers and writers are exiled, they lie sick in distant lands,
The cause is asleep, the strongest throats are choked with their own
   blood,

The young men droop their eyelashes toward the ground when they
    meet;
But for all this Liberty has not gone out of the place, nor the infidel
    enter'd into full possession.

When liberty goes out of a place it is not the first to go, nor the
    second or third to go,
It waits for all the rest to go, it is the last.

When there are no more memories of heroes and martyrs,
And when all life and all the souls of men and women are discharged
    from any part of the earth,
Then only shall liberty or the idea of liberty be discharged from that
    part of the earth,
And the infidel come into full possession.

Then courage European revolter, revoltress!
For till all ceases neither must you cease.

I do not know what you are for, (I do not know what I am for myself,
    nor what any thing is for,)
But I will search carefully for it even in being foil'd,
In defeat, poverty, misconception, imprisonment—for they too are great.

Did we think victory great?
So it is—but now it seems to me, when it cannot be help'd, that defeat
    is great,
And that death and dismay are great.

A Little Boy Lost

William Blake

Father, father, where are you going
   O do not walk so fast.
Speak father, speak to your little boy
   Or else I shall be lost,

The night was dark no father was there
   The child was wet with dew.
The mire was deep, & the child did weep
   And away the vapour flew.

The Wind that Shakes the Barley

Robert Dwyer Joyce

I sat within a valley green sat there with my true love
And my fond heart strove to choose between the old love and the
  new love
The old for her, the new that made me think on Ireland dearly
While soft the wind blew down the glade and shook the golden
  barley

'Twas hard the mournful words to frame to break the ties that bound
  us
Ah, but harder still to bear the shame of foreign chains around us
And so I said, 'The mountain glen I'll seek at morning early
And join the brave united men' while soft wind shook the barley

'Twas sad I kissed away her tears her arms around me clinging
When to my ears that fateful shot come out the wildwood ringing
The bullet pierced my true love's breast in life's young spring so early
And there upon my breast she died while soft wind shook the barley

I bore her to some mountain stream and many's the summer blossom
I placed with branches soft and green about her gore-stained bosom
I wept and kissed her clay-cold corpse then rushed o'er vale and
  valley
My vengeance on the foe to wreak while soft wind shook the barley

But blood for blood without remorse I've ta'en at Oulart Hollow
And placed my true love's clay-cold corpse where I full soon will follow
And round her grave I wander drear, noon, night and morning early
With breaking heart whene'er I hear the wind that shakes the barley!

Solidarity Song

Bertolt Brecht

Peoples of the world, together
Join to serve the common cause!
So it feeds us all for ever
See to it that it's now yours.

Forward, without forgetting
Where our strength can be seen now to be!
When starving or when eating
Forward, not forgetting
Our solidarity!

Black or white or brown or yellow
Leave your old disputes behind.
Once start talking with your fellow
Men, you'll soon be of one mind.

Forward, without forgetting
Where our strength can be seen now to be!
When starving or when eating
Forward, not forgetting
Our solidarity!

If we want to make this certain
We'll need you and your support.
It's yourselves you'll be deserting
if you rat your own sort.

Forward, without forgetting
Where our strength can be seen now to be!
When starving or when eating
Forward, not forgetting
Our solidarity!

All the gang of those who rule us
Hope our quarrels never stop
Helping them to split and fool us
So they can remain on top.

Forward, without forgetting
Where our strength can be seen now to be!
When starving or when eating
Forward, not forgetting
Our solidarity!

Workers of the world, uniting
That's the way to lose your chains.
Mighty regiments now are fighting
That no tyranny remains!

Forward, without forgetting
Till the concrete question is hurled
When starving or when eating:
Whose tomorrow is tomorrow?
And whose world is the world?

All Wi Doin is Defendin

Linton Kwesi Johnson

war . . . war . . .
mi seh lissen
oppressin man
hear what I say if yu can
wi have
a grevious blow fi blow

wi will fite yu in di street wid we han
wi have a plan
soh lissen man
get ready fi tek some blows

doze days
of di truncheon
an doze nites
of melancholy locked in a cell
doze hours of torture touchin hell
doze blows dat caused my heart to swell
were well
numbered
and are now
at an end

all wi doin
is defendin
soh get yu ready
fi war . . . war . . .
freedom is a very firm thing

all oppression
can do is bring
passion to di eights of eruption
an songs of fire wi will sing

no . . . no . . .
noh run
yu did soun yu siren
an is war now
war . . . war . . .

di Special Patrol
will fall
like a wall force doun
or a toun turn to dus
even dow dem think dem bold
wi know dem cold like ice wid fear
an wi is fire!
choose yu weapon dem
quick!
all wi need is bakkles an bricks an sticks
wi hav fist
wi fav feet
wi carry dandamite in wi teeth

sen fi di riot squad
quick!
cause wi runin wild

wi bittah like bile
blood will guide
their way
an I say
all wi doin
is defendin
soh set yu ready
fi war . . . war . . .
freedom is a very fine thing

Protest

Ella Wheeler Wilcox

To sin by silence, when we should protest,
Makes cowards out of men. The human race
Has climbed on protest. Had no voice been raised
Against injustice, ignorance, and lust,
The inquisition yet would serve the law,
And guillotines decide our least disputes.
The few who dare, must speak and speak again
To right the wrongs of many. Speech, thank God,
No vested power in this great day and land
Can gag or throttle. Press and voice may cry
Loud disapproval of existing ills;
May criticise oppression and condemn
The lawlessness of wealth-protecting laws
That let the children and childbearers toil
To purchase ease for idle millionaires.

Therefore I do protest against the boast
Of independence in this mighty land.
Call no chain strong, which holds one rusted link.
Call no land free, that holds one fettered slave.
Until the manacled slim wrists of babes
Are loosed to toss in childish sport and glee,
Until the mother bears no burden, save
The precious one beneath her heart, until
God's soil is rescued from the clutch of greed
And given back to labor, let no man
Call this the land of freedom.

4
Change

When we have said no it is easier for us to say yes. It is only after protest, after saying no, that we can say yes. The ultimate purpose of protest is change. But this change can be a change in the temperature of a society. It can represent an altered tone, a bringing to the fore of concerns previously unheard. It is in a way a making visible. If protest is a making heard, change is a making visible, a making real. But with poetry these things are more ambiguous. Sometimes a poem is the change that is dreamed of. Sometimes a poem breathes forth that change in images of the future. Not any particular future but the always hoped for future. It is a future that always remains relevant. It is never achieved in one time or another. For that would point to a perfected society. And we are always far from a perfected society here among flawed human beings. If humans ran heaven it would quickly become imperfect. We would choose our own kind to get in. That is perhaps why poems that hint at change always summon that change all through the ages. The best poems therefore address a particular time in a way that addresses all time. This intersection of the timely and the timeless is what characterises them. The embodiment of change can be in a tranquillity of tone; it can be in the solidity of an image; it can be in a mode of prophecy that sees the inevitability of rising after a fall. It can be in the secret structure of the metre itself.

But change is a mysterious thing. Sometimes a condition in society can seem so entrenched that it looks as if it would be that way forever. If you read the literature of feudalism it seemed that it would be the eternal condition of human beings. Apartheid in South Africa looked as if nothing could ever bring about its end. That night seemed destined to be always there in living history.

Even the Berlin Wall once seemed as eternal as death. Human yearning for change chipped away invisibly at the foundations that held up those structures. The more they seemed an eternal certainty the more they were passing away. It is just that no one saw it. The change that was happening was invisible. But true change, lasting change, is always invisible. That is perhaps because true change must happen in the invisible realm where that which must be changed was created in the first place. Change must happen in the mysterious realm of thought, of dreams, of yearnings, of will, of the spirit.

The atmosphere must change before the world can change. Those who aim at changing things themselves always fail, and the world reverts back to the changed thing. If change does not take place at the root of things, then it is never lasting change. This is where poetry is so powerful. The best poems speak to the root of things, shift the tone of the atmosphere, infect the oppressive system with bacteria of light. Perhaps things must be altered in the secret world before they are altered in the daylight world. Poetry speaks to that secret world. That is perhaps why a poem from three hundred years ago can still quietly undermine oppressive structures today. They infect the darkness. They plant possibility in what seems like an unchanging condition. Something may be there for hundreds of years and then one day its foundation is no longer secure. On another day it mysteriously crumbles. And what seemed like a fortress now becomes a ruin, a pile of stones. Empires and tyrannies have vanished thus beneath the secret force of change.

Poems of change are allied with this secret force that is almost a goddess. When Auden said that a poem never stopped a bullet he was perhaps too mesmerised by the facade of brute force. In his poems he knew that there are other forces. They don't stop bullets, they don't physically tear down tyrannies, but they do something just as potent and inevitable. They move the times forward. They accelerate the quiet collapse of impregnable structures. They do it through the spirit.

And sometimes poets go to jail or are tortured or exiled for breathing forth the dreamed of change. Sometimes they perish for it. But once the poems enter the world and work their way in the undergrowth, in time they join with other forces and help shift the axis of the world. Poems rarely change things themselves. But they help. They lend a constant shoulder.

St Crispin's Day

William Shakespeare

KING HENRY V
What's he that wishes so?
My cousin Westmoreland? No, my fair cousin;
If we are mark'd to die, we are enow
To do our country loss; and if to live,
The fewer men, the greater share of honour.
God's will! I pray thee, wish not one man more.
By Jove, I am not covetous for gold,
Nor care I who doth feed upon my cost;
It yearns me not if men my garments wear;
Such outward things dwell not in my desires.
But if it be a sin to covet honour,
I am the most offending soul alive.
No, faith, my coz, wish not a man from England.
God's peace! I would not lose so great an honour
As one man more, methinks, would share from me
For the best hope I have. O, do not wish one more!
Rather proclaim it, Westmoreland, through my host,
That he which hath no stomach to this fight,
Let him depart; his passport shall be made,
And crowns for convoy put into his purse;
We would not die in that man's company
That fears his fellowship to die with us.
This day is call'd the feast of Crispian.
He that outlives this day, and comes safe home,
Will stand a tip-toe when this day is nam'd,
And rouse him at the name of Crispian.
He that shall live this day, and see old age,

Will yearly on the vigil feast his neighbours,
And say 'To-morrow is Saint Crispian.'
Then will he strip his sleeve and show his scars,
And say 'These wounds I had on Crispian's day.'
Old men forget; yet all shall be forgot,
But he'll remember, with advantages,
What feats he did that day. Then shall our names,
Familiar in his mouth as household words,—
Harry the King, Bedford and Exeter,
Warwick and Talbot, Salisbury and Gloucester,—
Be in their flowing cups freshly remember'd.
This story shall the good man teach his son;
And Crispin Crispian shall ne'er go by,
From this day to the ending of the world,
But we in it shall be remembered,—
We few, we happy few, we band of brothers;
For he to-day that sheds his blood with me
Shall be my brother; be he ne'er so vile,
This day shall gentle his condition;
And gentlemen in England now-a-bed
Shall think themselves accurs'd they were not here,
And hold their manhoods cheap whiles any speaks
That fought with us upon Saint Crispin's day.

The Triumph of the Machine

D.H. Lawrence

They talk of triumph of the machine,
but the machine will never triumph.

Out of the thousands and thousands of centuries of man
the unrolling of ferns, white tongues of the acanthus lapping at the
   sun,
for one sad century
machines have triumphed, rolled us hither and thither,
shaking the lark's nest till the eggs have broken.
Shaken the marshes till the geese have gone
and the wild swans flown away singing the swan-song of us.

Hard, hard on the earth the machines are rolling,
but through some hearts they will never roll.

The lark nests in his heart
and the white swan swims in the marshes of his loins,
and through the wide prairies of his breast a young bull herds his
   cows,
lambs frisk among the daisies of his brain.

And at last
all these creatures that cannot die, driven back
into the uttermost corners of the soul,
will send up the wild cry of despair.

The thrilling lark in a wild despair will trill down arrows from the
   sky,

the swan will beat the waters in rage, white rage of an enraged
   swan,
even the lambs will stretch forth their necks like serpents,
like snakes of hate, against the man in the machine:
even the shaking white poplar will dazzle like splinters of glass against
   him.

And against this inward revolt of the native creatures of the soul
mechanical man, in triumph seated upon the seat of his machine
will be powerless, for no engine can reach into the marshes and
   depths of a man.

So mechanical man in triumph seated upon the seat of his machine
will be driven mad from within himself, and sightless, and on that
   day
the machines will turn to run into one another
traffic will tangle up in a long-drawn-out crash of collision
and engines will rush at the solid houses, the edifice of our life
will rock in the shock of the mad machine, and the house will come
   down.

Then, far beyond the ruin, in the far, in the ultimate, remote places
the swan will lift up again his flattened, smitten head
and look round, and rise, and on the great vaults of his wings
will sweep round and up to greet the sun with a silky glitter of a
   new day
and the lark will follow trilling, angerless again,
and the lambs will bite off the heads of the daisies for very friskiness.

But over the middle of the earth will be the smoky ruin of iron
the triumph of the machine.

Canto XII: From the Heights of Machu Picchu

Pablo Neruda

Rise up and be born with me, brother.
From the deepest reaches of your
disseminated sorrow, give me your hand.
You will not return from the depths of rock.
You will not return from subterranean time.
It will not return, your hardened voice.
They will not return, your drilled-out eyes.
Look at me from the depths of the earth,
ploughman, weaver, silent shepherd:
tender of the guardian guanacos:
mason of the impossible scaffold:
water-bearer of Andean tears:
goldsmith of crushed fingers:
farmer trembling on the seed:
potter poured out into your clay:
bring all your old buried sorrows
to the cup of this new life.
Show me your blood and your furrow,
say to me: here I was punished
because the gem didn't shine or the earth
didn't deliver the stone or the grain on time:
point out to me the rock on which you fell
and the wood on which they crucified you,
burn the ancient flints bright for me,
the ancient lamps, the lashing whips
stuck for centuries to your wounds
and the axes brilliant with bloodstain.
I come to speak through your dead mouth.

Through the earth unite all
the silent and split lips
and from the depths speak to me all night long
as if we were anchored together,
tell me everything, chain by chain,
link by link and step by step,
sharpen the knives you kept,
place them in my chest and in my hand,
like a river of yellow lightning,
like a river of buried jaguars,
and let me weep, hours, days, years,
blind ages, stellar centuries.

Give me silence, water, hope.

Give me struggle, iron, volcanoes.

Fasten your bodies to mine like magnets.

Come to my veins and my mouth.

Speak through my words and my blood.

The Age Demanded

Ernest Hemingway

The age demanded that we sing
And cut away our tongue.

The age demanded that we flow
And hammered in the bung.

The age demanded that we dance
And jammed us into iron pants.

And in the end the age was handed
The sort of shit that it demanded.

The Gadfly

John Keats

1.

All gentle folks who owe a grudge
To any living thing
Open your ears and stay your trudge
Whilst I in dudgeon sing.

2.

The Gadfly he hath stung me sore—
O may he ne'er sting you!
But we have many a horrid bore
He may sting black and blue.

3.

Has any here an old grey Mare
With three legs all her store,
O put it to her Buttocks bare
And straight she'll run on four.

4.

Has any here a Lawyer suit
Of Seventeen-Forty-Three,
Take Lawyer's nose and put it to't
And you the end will see.

5.

Is there a Man in Parliament
Dum[b-] founder'd in his speech,
O let his neighbour make a rent
And put one in his breech.

6.

O Lowther how much better thou
Hadst figur'd t'other day
When to the folks thou mad'st a bow
And hadst no more to say.

7.

If lucky Gadfly had but ta'en
His seat * * * * * * * * *
And put thee to a little pain
To save thee from a worse.

8.

Better than Southey it had been,
Better than Mr D———,
Better than Wordsworth too, I ween,
Better than Mr V———.

9.

Forgive me pray good people all
For deviating so—
In spirit sure I had a call—
And now I on will go.

10.

Has any here a daughter fair
Too fond of reading novels,

Too apt to fall in love with care
And charming Mister Lovels,

11.
O put a Gadfly to that thing
She keeps so white and pert—
I mean the finger for the ring,
And it will breed a wort.

12.
Has any here a pious spouse
Who seven times a day
Scolds as King David pray'd, to chouse
And have her holy way—

13.
O let a Gadfly's little sting
Persuade her sacred tongue
That noises are a common thing,
But that her bell has rung.

14.
And as this is the summum bo
num of all conquering,
I leave 'withouten wordes mo'
The Gadfly's little sting.

Give your soul to the hungry

Isaiah 58: 7–8

7 Is it not to deal thy bread
   to the hungry,
   and that thou bring the poor
   that are cast out to thy house?
   when thou seest the naked,
   that thou cover him;
   and that thou hide not thyself
   from thine own flesh?

8 Then shall thy light break
   forth as the morning,
   and thine health shall spring
   forth speedily:
   and thy righteousness
   shall go before thee;
   the glory of the Lord
   shall be thy reward.

I Shall Vote Labour

Christopher Logue

I shall vote Labour because
God votes Labour.
I shall vote Labour to protect
the sacred institution of The Family.
I shall vote Labour because
I am a dog.
I shall vote Labour because
upper-class hoorays annoy me in expensive restaurants.
I shall vote Labour because
I am on a diet.
I shall vote Labour because if I don't
somebody else will:
AND
I shall vote Labour because if one person
does it
everybody will be wanting to do it.
I shall vote Labour because if I do not vote Labour
my balls will drop off.
I shall vote Labour because
there are too few cars on the road.
I shall vote Labour because I am
a hopeless drug addict.
I shall vote Labour because
I failed to be a dollar millionaire aged three.
I shall vote Labour because Labour will build
more maximum security prisons.
I shall vote Labour because I want to shop
in an all-weather precinct stretching from Yeovil

to Glasgow.
I shall vote Labour because
the Queen's stamp collection is the best
in the world.
I shall vote Labour because
deep in my heart
I am a Conservative.

Ode to Liberty

Percy Bysshe Shelley

Yet, Freedom, yet, thy banner, torn but flying,
Streams like a thunder-storm against the wind.—Byron.

I.
A glorious people vibrated again
The lightning of the nations: Liberty
From heart to heart, from tower to tower, o'er Spain,
Scattering contagious fire into the sky,
Gleamed. My soul spurned the chains of its dismay,
And in the rapid plumes of song
Clothed itself, sublime and strong;
As a young eagle soars the morning clouds among,
Hovering inverse o'er its accustomed prey;
Till from its station in the Heaven of fame
The Spirit's whirlwind rapped it, and the ray
Of the remotest sphere of living flame
Which paves the void was from behind it flung,
As foam from a ship's swiftness, when there came
A voice out of the deep: I will record the same.

***

III.
Man, the imperial shape, then multiplied
His generations under the pavilion
Of the Sun's throne: palace and pyramid,
Temple and prison, to many a swarming million
Were, as to mountain-wolves their ragged caves.
This human living multitude
Was savage, cunning, blind, and rude,

For thou wert not; but o'er the populous solitude,
Like one fierce cloud over a waste of waves,
Hung Tyranny; beneath, sate deified
The sister-pest, congregator of slaves;
Into the shadow of her pinions wide
Anarchs and priests, who feed on gold and blood
Till with the stain their inmost souls are dyed,
Drove the astonished herds of men from every side.

***

XV.
Oh, that the free would stamp the impious name
Of KING into the dust! or write it there,
So that this blot upon the page of fame
Were as a serpent's path, which the light air
Erases, and the flat sands close behind!
Ye the oracle have heard:
Lift the victory-flashing sword.
And cut the snaky knots of this foul gordian word,
Which, weak itself as stubble, yet can bind
Into a mass, irrefragably firm,
The axes and the rods which awe mankind;
The sound has poison in it, 'tis the sperm
Of what makes life foul, cankerous, and abhorred;
Disdain not thou, at thine appointed term,
To set thine armed heel on this reluctant worm.

XVI.

Oh, that the wise from their bright minds would kindle
Such lamps within the dome of this dim world,
That the pale name of PRIEST might shrink and dwindle
Into the hell from which it first was hurled,
A scoff of impious pride from fiends impure;
Till human thoughts might kneel alone,
Each before the judgement-throne
Of its own aweless soul, or of the Power unknown!
Oh, that the words which make the thoughts obscure
From which they spring, as clouds of glimmering dew
From a white lake blot Heaven's blue portraiture,
Were stripped of their thin masks and various hue
And frowns and smiles and splendours not their own,
Till in the nakedness of false and true
They stand before their Lord, each to receive its due!

XVII.

He who taught man to vanquish whatsoever
Can be between the cradle and the grave
Crowned him the King of Life. Oh, vain endeavour!
If on his own high will, a willing slave,
He has enthroned the oppression and the oppressor
What if earth can clothe and feed
Amplest millions at their need,
And power in thought be as the tree within the seed?
Or what if Art, an ardent intercessor,
Driving on fiery wings to Nature's throne,

Checks the great mother stooping to caress her,
And cries: 'Give me, thy child, dominion
Over all height and depth'? if Life can breed
New wants, and wealth from those who toil and groan,
Rend of thy gifts and hers a thousandfold for one!

XVIII.
Come thou, but lead out of the inmost cave
Of man's deep spirit, as the morning-star
Beckons the Sun from the Eoan wave,
Wisdom. I hear the pennons of her car
Self-moving, like cloud charioted by flame;
Comes she not, and come ye not,
Rulers of eternal thought,
To judge, with solemn truth, life's ill-apportioned lot?
Blind Love, and equal Justice, and the Fame
Of what has been, the Hope of what will be?
O Liberty! if such could be thy name
Wert thou disjoined from these, or they from thee:
If thine or theirs were treasures to be bought
By blood or tears, have not the wise and free
Wept tears, and blood like tears?—The solemn harmony

XIX.
Paused, and the Spirit of that mighty singing
To its abyss was suddenly withdrawn;
Then, as a wild swan, when sublimely winging
Its path athwart the thunder-smoke of dawn,

Sinks headlong through the aereal golden light
On the heavy-sounding plain,
When the bolt has pierced its brain;
As summer clouds dissolve, unburthened of their rain;
As a far taper fades with fading night,
As a brief insect dies with dying day,—
My song, its pinions disarrayed of might,
Drooped; o'er it closed the echoes far away
Of the great voice which did its flight sustain,
As waves which lately paved his watery way
Hiss round a drowner's head in their tempestuous play.

Emperors and Kings, How Oft Have Temples Rung

William Wordsworth

Emperors and Kings, how oft have temples rung
With impious thanksgiving, the Almighty's scorn!
How oft above their altars have been hung
Trophies that led the good and wise to mourn
Triumphant wrong, battle of battle born,
And sorrow that to fruitless sorrow clung!
Now, from Heaven-sanctioned victory, Peace is sprung;
In this firm hour Salvation lifts her horn.
Glory to arms! But, conscious that the nerve
Of popular reason, long mistrusted, freed
Your thrones, ye Powers, from duty fear to swerve!
Be just, be grateful; nor, the oppressor's creed
Reviving, heavier chastisement deserve
Than ever forced unpitied hearts to bleed.

The Sower

Victor Hugo

Sitting in a porchway cool,
Fades the ruddy sunlight fast,
Twilight hastens on to rule—
Working hours are well-nigh past

Shadows shoot across the lands;
But one sower lingers still,
Old, in rags, he patient stands,—
Looking on, I feel a thrill.

Black and high his silhouette
Dominates the furrows deep!
Now to sow the task is set,
Soon shall come a time to reap.

Marches he along the plain,
To and fro, and scatters wide
From his hands the precious grain;
Moody, I, to see him stride.

Darkness deepens. Gone the light.
Now his gestures to mine eyes
Are august; and strange—his height
Seems to touch the starry skies.

The Tree of Liberty

Robert Burns

Heard ye o' the tree o' France,
I watna what's the name o't;
Around it a' the patriots dance,
Weel Europe kens the fame o't.
It stands where ance the Bastille stood,
A prison built by kings, man,
When Superstition's hellish brood
Kept France in leading-strings, man.

Upo' this tree there grows sic fruit,
Its virtues a' can tell, man;
It raises man aboon the brute,
It mak's him ken himsel, man.
Gif ance the peasant taste a bit,
He's greater than a lord, man,
An' wi' the beggar shares a mite
O' a' he can afford, man.

This fruit is worth a' Afric's wealth:
To comfort us 'twas sent, man:
To gie the sweetest blush o' health,
An' mak us a' content, man.
It clears the een, it cheers the heart,
Maks high and low gude friends, man;
And he wha acts the traitor's part,
It to perdition sends, man.

My blessings aye attend the chiel
Wha pitied Gallia's slaves, man,
And staw a branch, spite o' the deil,
Frae yont the western waves, man.
Fair Virtue water'd it wi' care,
And now she sees wi' pride, man,
How weel it buds and blossoms there,
Its branches spreading wide, man.

But vicious folk aye hate to see
The works o' Virtue thrive, man;
The courtly vermin's bann'd the tree,
And grat to see it thrive, man;
King Loui' thought to cut it down,
When it was unco sma', man;
For this the watchman crack'd his crown,
Cut aff his head and a', man.

A wicked crew syne, on a time,
Did tak a solemn aith, man,
It ne'er should flourish to its prime,
I wat they pledged their faith, man.
Awa' they gaed wi' mock parade,
Like beagles hunting game, man,
But soon grew weary o' the trade
And wished they'd been at hame, man.

For Freedom, standing by the tree,
Her sons did loudly ca', man.
She sang a sang o' liberty,
Which pleased them ane and a', man.
By her inspired, the new-born race
Soon drew the avenging steel, man;
The hirelings ran—her foes gied chase,
And banged the despot weel, man.

Let Britain boast her hardy oak,
Her poplar and her pine, man,
Auld Britain ance could crack her joke,
And o'er her neighbours shine, man.
But seek the forest round and round,
And soon 'twill be agreed, man,
That sic a tree can not be found,
'Twixt London and the Tweed, man.

Without this tree alake this life
Is but a vale o' woe, man;
A scene o' sorrow mixed wi' strife,
Nae real joys we know, man.
We labour soon, we labour late,
To feed the titled knave, man;
And a' the comfort we're to get,
Is that ayont the grave, man.

Wi' plenty o' sic trees, I trow,
The warld would live in peace, man;
The sword would help to mak a plough,
The din o' war wad cease, man.
Like brethren in a common cause,
We'd on each other smile, man;
And equal rights and equal laws
Wad gladden every isle, man.

Wae worth the loon wha wadna eat
Sic halesome dainty cheer, man;
I'd gie the shoon frae aff my feet,
To taste sic fruit, I SWEAR, man.
Syne let us pray, auld England may
Sure plant this far-famed tree, man;
And blythe we'll sing, and hail the day
That gives us liberty, man.

Do not forget the plum

Matsuo Basho

Do not forget the plum,
blooming
in the thicket.

Work

Kahlil Gibran

Then a ploughman said, 'Speak to us of Work.'
And he answered, saying:
You work that you may keep pace with the earth and the soul of the earth.
For to be idle is to become a stranger unto the seasons,
and to step out of life's procession, that marches in majesty and proud submission towards the infinite.

When you work you are a flute through whose heart the whispering of the hours turns to music.
Which of you would be a reed, dumb and silent, when all else sings together in unison?

Always you have been told that work is a curse and labour a misfortune.
But I say to you that when you work you fulfil a part of earth's furthest dream, assigned to you when that dream was born,
And in keeping yourself with labour you are in truth loving life,
And to love life through labour is to be intimate with life's inmost secret.

But if you in your pain call birth an affliction and the support of the flesh
a curse written upon your brow, then I answer that naught but the sweat of your brow shall wash away that which is written.

You have been told also that life is darkness, and in your weariness you echo what was said by the weary.
And I say that life is indeed darkness save when there is urge,
And all urge is blind save when there is knowledge,

And all knowledge is vain save when there is work,
And all work is empty save when there is love;
And when you work with love you bind yourself to yourself, and to one another, and to God.

And what is it to work with love?
It is to weave the cloth with threads drawn from your heart,
even as if your beloved were to wear that cloth.
It is to build a house with affection,
even as if your beloved were to dwell in that house.
It is to sow seeds with tenderness and reap the harvest with joy,
even as if your beloved were to eat the fruit.
It is to charge all things you fashion with a breath of your own spirit,
And to know that all the blessed dead
are standing about you and watching.

Often have I heard you say, as if speaking in sleep, 'He who works in marble, and finds the shape of his own soul in the stone, is nobler than he who ploughs the soil.
And he who seizes the rainbow to lay it on a cloth in the likeness of man,
is more than he who makes the sandals for our feet.'
But I say, not in sleep but in the over-wakefulness of noontide, that the wind speaks not more sweetly to the giant oaks than to the least of all the blades of grass;
And he alone is great who turns the voice of the wind into a song made sweeter by his own loving.

Work is love made visible.

And if you cannot work with love but only with distaste, it is better that you should leave your work and sit at the gate of the temple and take alms of those who work with joy.

For if you bake bread with indifference, you bake a bitter bread that feeds
but half man's hunger.

And if you grudge the crushing of the grapes, your grudge distils a poison in the wine.

And if you sing though as angels, and love not the singing, you muffle man's ears to the voices of the day and the voices of the night.

Revolution is the Pod

Emily Dickinson

Revolution is the Pod
Systems rattle from
When the Winds of Will are stirred
Excellent is Bloom

But except its Russet Base
Every Summer be
The Entomber of itself,
So of Liberty—

Left inactive on the Stalk
All its Purple fled
Revolution shakes it for
Test if it be dead.

Reality Demands

Wisława Szymborska

Reality demands
we also state the following:
life goes on.
At Cannae and Borodino,
at Kosovo Polje and in Guernica.

There is a gas station
in a small plaza in Jericho,
and freshly painted
benches near Bila Hora.
Letters travel
between Pearl Harbor and Hastings,
a furniture truck passes
before the eyes of the lion of Chaeronea,
and only an atmospheric front advances
toward the blossoming orchards near Verdun.

There is so much of Everything,
that Nothing is quite well concealed.
Music flows
from yachts at Actium
and on board couples dance in the sun.

So much keeps happening,
that it must be happening everywhere.
Where not a stone is left standing,
there is an ice-cream truck
besieged by children.

Where Hiroshima had been,
Hiroshima is again
manufacturing products
for everyday use.

Not without its draws is this terrible world,
not without its dawns
worth our waking.

In the fields of Maciejowice
the grass is green
and on the grass is—you know how grass is—
transparent dew.

Maybe there are no fields but battlefields,
those still remembered,
and those long forgotten,
birch groves and cedar groves,
snows and sands, iridescent swamps,
and ravines of dark defeat
where today, in sudden need,
you squat behind a bush.

What moral flows from this? Probably none.
But what really flows is quickly drying blood,
and as always, some rivers and clouds.

On the tragic mountain passes
the wind blows hats off heads
and we cannot help—
but laugh.

Eclogue IV

Virgil

Muses of Sicily, essay we now
A somewhat loftier task! Not all men love
Coppice or lowly tamarisk: sing we woods,
Woods worthy of a Consul let them be.
Now the last age by Cumae's Sibyl sung
Has come and gone, and the majestic roll
Of circling centuries begins anew:
Justice returns, returns old Saturn's reign,
With a new breed of men sent down from heaven.
Only do thou, at the boy's birth in whom
The iron shall cease, the golden race arise,
Befriend him, chaste Lucina; 'tis thine own
Apollo reigns. And in thy consulate,
This glorious age, O Pollio, shall begin,
And the months enter on their mighty march.
Under thy guidance, whatso tracks remain
Of our old wickedness, once done away,
Shall free the earth from never-ceasing fear.
He shall receive the life of gods, and see
Heroes with gods commingling, and himself
Be seen of them, and with his father's worth
Reign o'er a world at peace. For thee, O boy,
First shall the earth, untilled, pour freely forth
Her childish gifts, the gadding ivy-spray
With foxglove and Egyptian bean-flower mixed,
And laughing-eyed acanthus. Of themselves,
But in the meadows shall the ram himself,
Now with soft flush of purple, now with tint

Of yellow saffron, teach his fleece to shine.
While clothed in natural scarlet graze the lambs.
"Such still, such ages weave ye, as ye run,"
Sang to their spindles the consenting Fates
By Destiny's unalterable decree.
Assume thy greatness, for the time draws high,
Dear child of gods, great progeny of Jove!
See how it totters- the world's orbed might,
Earth and wide ocean, and the vault profound,
All, see, enraptured of the coming time!
Ah! might such length of days to me be given,
And breath suffice me to rehearse thy deeds,
Nor Thracian Orpheus should out-sing me then,
Nor Linus, through his mother this, and that
His sire should aid- Orpheus Calliope,
And Linus fair Apollo. Nay, though pan,
With Arcady for judge, my claim contest,
With Arcady for judge great Pan himself
Should own him foiled, and from the field retire.
Begin to greet thy mother with a smile,
O baby-boy! ten months of weariness
For thee she bore: O baby-boy, begin!
For him, on whom his parents have not smiled,
Gods deem not worthy of their board or bed.

A Worker Reads History

Bertolt Brecht

Who built the seven gates of Thebes?
The books are filled with names of kings.
Was it the kings who hauled the craggy blocks of stone?
And Babylon, so many times destroyed.
Who built the city up each time? In which of Lima's houses,
That city glittering with gold, lived those who built it?
In the evening when the Chinese wall was finished
Where did the masons go? Imperial Rome
Is full of arcs of triumph. Who reared them up? Over whom
Did the Caesars triumph? Byzantium lives in song.
Were all her dwellings palaces? And even in Atlantis of the legend
The night the seas rushed in,
The drowning men still bellowed for their slaves.

Young Alexander conquered India.
He alone?
Caesar beat the Gauls.
Was there not even a cook in his army?
Phillip of Spain wept as his fleet
was sunk and destroyed. Were there no other tears?
Frederick the Great triumphed in the Seven Years War.
Who triumphed with him?

Each page a victory
At whose expense the victory ball?
Every ten years a great man,
Who paid the piper?

So many particulars.
So many questions.

Ithaka

C.P. Cavafy

As you set out for Ithaka
hope your road is a long one,
full of adventure, full of discovery.
Laistrygonians, Cyclops,
angry Poseidon—don't be afraid of them:
you'll never find things like that on your way
as long as you keep your thoughts raised high,
as long as a rare excitement
stirs your spirit and your body.
Laistrygonians, Cyclops,
wild Poseidon—you won't encounter them
unless you bring them along inside your soul,
unless your soul sets them up in front of you.

Hope your road is a long one.
May there be many summer mornings when,
with what pleasure, what joy,
you enter harbours you're seeing for the first time;
may you stop at Phoenician trading stations
to buy fine things,
mother of pearl and coral, amber and ebony,
sensual perfume of every kind—
as many sensual perfumes as you can;
and may you visit many Egyptian cities
to learn and go on learning from their scholars.

Keep Ithaka always in your mind.
Arriving there is what you're destined for.

But don't hurry the journey at all.
Better if it lasts for years,
so you're old by the time you reach the island,
wealthy with all you've gained on the way,
not expecting Ithaka to make you rich.

Ithaka gave you the marvellous journey.
Without her you wouldn't have set out.
She has nothing left to give you now.

And if you find her poor, Ithaka won't have fooled you.
Wise as you will have become, so full of experience,
you'll have understood by then what these Ithakas mean.

Spain, Take this Cup Away From Me

César Vallejo

Children of the earth,
if Spain falls—I say, it's a manner of speaking—
if there should fall
down from the sky her forearm, which is seized
and pulled along by two earth-forged plates;
children, what an age of sunken temples!
How early in the sun what I was telling you!
How soon within your breast the ancient clamour!
How old your 2 in the quarto.

Children of the earth, here is
Mother Spain with her belly on her back!
Here is our teacher with her yardstick,
she is mother and teacher,
cross and timber, because she gave you the height,
vertigo and division and sum, children
it's up to her, fathers of due process.

If she falls—I say, it's a manner of speaking—If Spain
falls, from the earth downwards,
children! How you are going to stop growing!
How the year is going to punish the month,
how your teeth will be limited to ten,
the diphthong yoked, the medal in tears.
How the little lamb will go on
being tied by the hoof to the great inkwell.
How you are going to go down the steps of the alphabet
to the letter in which grief was born.

Children,
sons of warriors, meanwhile,
lower your voice, since Spain at this very moment is dividing
her energy among the animal kingdom,
the tiny flowers, the comets and men.
Lower your voice, for she is
with her rigour, which is great, not knowing
what to do, and there in her hand
is the skull speaking and talk and talk
the skull, that one with the braid,
the skull, that one that's alive!

Lower your voice, I bid you;
lower your voice, the song of the syllables, the weeping
of matter and the minor hum of the pyramids, and even
that of the temples that walk with two stones!
Lower your breath, and if
your forearm drops,
if the yardsticks ring, if it is night,
if the heavens fit between two terrestrial limbos,
if there is noise in the sound of doors,
if I delay,
if you don't see anyone, if you are alarmed
by pencils without points, if mother
Spain falls—I say, it's a manner of speaking—
go out, children of the earth, go and seek her!

The Hand That Signed the Paper

Dylan Thomas

The hand that signed the paper felled a city;
Five sovereign fingers taxed the breath,
Doubled the globe of dead and halved a country;
These five kings did a king to death.

The mighty hand leads to a sloping shoulder,
The finger joints are cramped with chalk;
A goose's quill has put an end to murder
That put an end to talk.

The hand that signed the treaty bred a fever,
And famine grew, and locusts came;
Great is the hand that holds dominion over
Man by a scribbled name.

The five kings count the dead but do not soften
The crusted wound nor stroke the brow;
A hand rules pity as a hand rules heaven;
Hands have no tears to flow.

The Trial of a Man

Sylvia Plath

The ordinary milkman brought that dawn
Of destiny, delivered to the door
In square hermetic bottles, while the sun
Ruled decree of doomsday on the floor.

The morning paper clocked the headline hour
You drank your coffee like original sin,
And at the jet-plane anger of God's roar
Got up to let the suave blue policeman in.

Impaled upon a stern angelic stare
You were condemned to serve the legal limit
And burn to death within your neon hell.

Now, disciplined in the strict ancestral chair,
You sit, solemn-eyed, about to vomit,
The future an electrode in your skull.

Big Yellow Taxi

Joni Mitchell

They paved paradise
And put up a parking lot
With a pink hotel, a boutique
And a swinging hot spot

Don't it always seem to go
That you don't know what you've got
Till it's gone
They paved paradise
And put up a parking lot

They took all the trees
Put 'em in a tree museum
And they charged all the people
A dollar and a half just to see 'em

Don't it always seem to go
That you don't know what you've got
Till it's gone
They paved paradise
And put up a parking lot

Hey farmer farmer
Put away that DDT now
Give me spots on my apples
But leave me the birds and the bees
Please!

Don't it always seem to go
That you don't know what you've got
Till it's gone
They paved paradise
And put up a parking lot

Late last night
I heard the screen door slam
And a big yellow taxi
Took away my old man

Don't it always seem to go
That you don't know what you've got
Till it's gone
They paved paradise
And put up a parking lot

They paved paradise
And put up a parking lot

The Glories of Our Blood and State

James Shirley

The glories of our blood and state
   Are shadows, not substantial things;
There is no armour against Fate;
   Death lays his icy hand on kings:
      Sceptre and Crown
      Must tumble down,
And in the dust be equal made
With the poor crooked scythe and spade.

Some men with swords may reap the field,
   And plant fresh laurels where they kill:
But their strong nerves at last must yield;
   They tame but one another still:
      Early or late
      They stoop to fate,
And must give up their murmuring breath
When they, pale captives, creep to death.

The garlands wither on your brow;
   Then boast no more your mighty deeds!
Upon Death's purple altar now
   See where the victor-victim bleeds.
      Your heads must come
      To the cold tomb:
Only the actions of the just
Smell sweet and blossom in their dust.

5
Truth

Ultimately poetry transcends. It speaks beyond. It speaks at, but it also speaks beyond. It gathers all our inner states, the core of our being, and it takes us beyond. That beyond is not somewhere far off, it is not a visionary land. It is here. It takes us to the core of here, to the truth of now.

Before protest there is truth. Before the conditions that make us abandon beauty for a while, to lift up our voices against that which insults our dignity, that which oppresses us, that which deprives us of hope, before all of that there was truth. It speaks to the condition before injustice was perceived and it speaks to the condition after we have taken up the arms of our spirit and our voices against that injustice. Poetry that embodies this truth reminds us of core things, of those eternal verities that transcend left or right, this or that, your side and my side. It speaks to the human in us, and when we get carried away with the certainty of our cause, and veer with our sense of justice too far from the human truths, it reminds us that sometimes justice is not everything. It reminds us that beneath our differences, beneath our oppositions, something mysterious unites us that is greater than our dissensions and divisions. Sometimes even justice can be too stern, and the highest causes need the leavening of the human. You may think of it as the third point of a triangle, uniting this way and that way, heaven and earth, left and right, extreme individualism and extreme socialism. You may also think of it as something beyond any one side, truer than either, true as the sea, true as the wind on our faces, true as the peace on the face of a sleeping child, true as the rose, the storm, or the heron in flight.

Sometimes the truth of a condition is not what the mind thinks. Sometimes when the heart is stilled the truth rises up in our souls, and it is beyond words. We feel it in our bones and in our breathing. No laws written by man or woman can legislate this knowledge that rises up in us from the deep roots of our unsuspected humanity. In moments like that we do something that transcends our political inclination or even the narrow bounds of our temperaments. Those moments perhaps are when history touches or is touched by the transcendent and ever afterwards are causes of wonder, beyond explication. Those are the moments in art or culture, in history or in society, that give the special meaning to the word civilisation. Those moments give the glamour and the imaginative force to the mass of moments in which we were less than ourselves, in which we quarrelled, raged, quibbled and disagreed. These moments cast a sheen on all that tempest of spirit and render time amongst one another fit for narration, for poetry.

These poems are always true. In the midst of the struggle, they are true. When the struggle is over, if it can ever be over, they are still true. They are the melodic line that runs in the bones of our striving and our temporary peace. For there is never any end to the struggle of humanity towards truth and fairness and justice. Not until justice and the goodness of life are universal, not until there is an end to poverty, not until every human being knows the dignity of being human, and is not under any oppression of hunger or inequality, can there be any end to the struggle of the soul for the blessing of the sun and the joyful laughter of being alive. It is only through the struggle that we each render our truths to one another. Power ought to exist to elevate the human, to help each and every one of us to achieve our full potential and to make our best contribution to this great ongoing story of civilisation.

But when power fails to listen, when it insults our humanity, we have no choice. Guided by light and truth and the poetry of being, we have no choice then but to rise like lions.

The Return of The Proconsul

Zbigniew Herbert

I've decided to return to the emperor's court
once more I shall see if it's possible to live there
I could stay here in this remote province
under the full sweet leaves of the sycamore
and the gentle rule of sickly nepotists

when I return I don't intend to commend myself
I shall applaud in measured portions
smile in ounces frown discreetly
for that they will not give me a golden chain
this iron one will suffice

I've decided to return tomorrow or the day after
I cannot live among vineyards nothing here is mine
trees have no roots houses no foundations the rain is
    glassy flowers smell of wax
a dry cloud rattles against the empty sky
so I shall return tomorrow or the day after in any case I shall
    return

I must come to terms with my face again
with my lower lip so it knows how to curb its scorn
with my eyes so they remain ideally empty
and with that miserable chin the hare of my face
which trembles when the chief of guards walks in

of one thing I am sure I will not drink wine with him
when he brings his goblet nearer I will lower my eyes

and pretend I'm picking bits of food from between my teeth
besides the emperor likes courage of convictions
to a certain extent to a certain reasonable extent
he is after all a man like everyone else

and already tired by all those tricks with poison
he cannot drink his fill incessant chess
this left cup is for Drusus from the right one pretend to sip
then drink only water never lose sight of Tacitus
go out into the garden and come back when they've taken
    away the corpse

I've decided to return to the emperor's court
yes I hope that things will work out somehow

Death Fugue

Paul Celan

Black milk of morning we drink you at dusktime
we drink you at noontime and dawntime we drink you at night
we drink and drink
we scoop out a grave in the sky where it's roomy to lie
There's a man in this house who cultivates snakes and who writes
who writes when it's nightfall *nach Deutschland* your golden hair
   Margareta
he writes it and walks from the house and the stars all start flashing
   he whistles his dogs to draw near
whistles his Jews to appear starts us scooping a grave out of sand
he commands us to play for the dance

Black milk of morning we drink you at night
we drink you at dawntime and noontime we drink you at dusktime
we drink and drink
There's a man in this house who cultivates snakes and who writes
who writes when it's nightfall *nach Deutschland* your golden hair
   Margareta
your ashen hair Shulamite we scoop out a grave in the sky where
   it's roomy to lie
He calls jab it deep in the soil you lot there you other men sing and
   play
he tugs at the sword in his belt he swings it his eyes are blue
jab your spades deeper you men you other men you others play up
   again for the dance

Black milk of morning we drink you at night
we drink you at noontime and dawntime we drink you at dusktime

we drink and drink
there's a man in this house your golden hair Margareta
your ashen hair Shulamite he cultivates snakes

He calls play that death thing more sweetly Death is a gang-boss *aus
Deutschland*
he calls scrape that fiddle more darkly then hover like smoke in the
air
then scoop out a grave in the clouds where it's roomy to lie

Black milk of morning we drink you at night
we drink you at noontime Death is a gang-boss *aus Deutschland*
we drink you at dusktime and dawntime we drink and drink
Death is a gang-boss *aus Deutschland* his eye is blue
he shoots you with leaden bullets his aim is true
there's a man in this house your golden hair Margareta
he sets his dogs on our trail he gives us a grave in the sky
he cultivates snakes and he dreams Death is a gang-boss *aus
Deutschland*

your golden hair Margareta
your ashen hair Shulamite

Belshazzar's Feast

Daniel 5: 17-30

17 Then Daniel answered
    and said before the king,
    Let thy gifts be to thyself,
    and give thy rewards to another;
    yet I will read the writing unto the king,
    and make known to him the interpretation.

18 O thou king, the most high God gave
    Nebuchadnezzar thy father a kingdom,
    and majesty, and glory,
       and honour:

19 And for the majesty that he gave him,
    all people, nations, and languages,
    trembled and feared before him:
    whom he would he slew;
    and whom he would he kept alive;
    and whom he would he set up;
    and whom he would he put down.

20 But when his heart was lifted up,
    and his mind hardened in pride,
    he was deposed from his kingly throne,
    and they took his glory from him:

21 And he was driven from the sons of men;
    and his heart was made like the beasts,
    and his dwelling was with the wild asses:

they fed him with grass like oxen,
and his body was wet with the dew of heaven;
till he knew that the most high God ruled
in the kingdom of men,
and that he appointeth over it
whomsoever he will.

22 And thou his son, O Belshazzar,
hast not humbled thine heart,
though thou knewest all this;

23 But hast lifted up thyself against
the Lord of heaven;
and they have brought the vessels
of his house before thee,
and thou, and thy lords, thy wives,
and thy concubines,
have drunk wine in them;
and thou hast praised the gods of silver,
and gold, of brass, iron, wood, and stone,
which see not, nor hear, nor know:
and the God in whose hand thy breath is,
and whose are all thy ways,
hast thou not glorified:

24 Then was the part of the hand
sent from him;
and this writing was written.

25 And this is the writing
   that was written,
   Mene, Mene, Tekel, Upharsin.

26 This is the interpretation
   of the thing:
   Mene; God hath numbered
   thy kingdom,
   and finished it.

27 Tekel; Thou art weighed
   in the balances,
   and art found wanting.

28 Peres; Thy kingdom
   is divided, and given
   to the Medes and Persians.

29 Then commanded Belshazzar,
   and they clothed Daniel
   with scarlet,
   and put a chain of gold
   about his neck,
   and made a proclamation
   concerning him,
   that he should be the third
   ruler in the kingdom.

30 In that night
was Belshazzar
the king
of the Chaldeans
slain.

To be or not to be

William Shakespeare

HAMLET
To be, or not to be—that is the question:
Whether 'tis nobler in the mind to suffer
The slings and arrows of outrageous fortune
Or to take arms against a sea of troubles
And by opposing end them. To die, to sleep—
No more—and by a sleep to say we end
The heartache, and the thousand natural shocks
That flesh is heir to. 'Tis a consummation
Devoutly to be wished. To die, to sleep—
To sleep—perchance to dream: ay, there's the rub,
For in that sleep of death what dreams may come
When we have shuffled off this mortal coil,
Must give us pause. There's the respect
That makes calamity of so long life.
For who would bear the whips and scorns of time,
Th' oppressor's wrong, the proud man's contumely
The pangs of despised love, the law's delay,
The insolence of office, and the spurns
That patient merit of th' unworthy takes,
When he himself might his quietus make
With a bare bodkin? Who would fardels bear,
To grunt and sweat under a weary life,
But that the dread of something after death,
The undiscovered country, from whose bourn
No traveller returns, puzzles the will,
And makes us rather bear those ills we have
Than fly to others that we know not of?

Thus conscience does make cowards of us all,
And thus the native hue of resolution
Is sicklied o'er with the pale cast of thought,
And enterprise of great pitch and moment
With this regard their currents turn awry
And lose the name of action.

Intimations of Immortality from Recollections of Early Childhood

William Wordsworth

There was a time when meadow, grove, and stream,
The earth, and every common sight
    To me did seem
  Apparelled in celestial light,
The glory and the freshness of a dream.
It is not now as it hath been of yore;—
  Turn wheresoe'er I may,
  By night or day,
The things which I have seen I now can see no more.

    The rainbow comes and goes,
    And lovely is the rose;
    The moon doth with delight
  Look round her when the heavens are bare;
    Waters on a starry night
    Are beautiful and fair;
  The sunshine is a glorious birth;
  But yet I know, where'er I go,
That there hath passed away a glory from the earth.

Now, while the birds thus sing a joyous song,
  And while the young lambs bound
    As to the tabor's sound,
To me alone there came a thought of grief:
A timely utterance gave that thought relief,
    And I again am strong.

The cataracts blow their trumpets from the steep,—
No more shall grief of mine the season wrong:
I hear the echoes through the mountains throng.
The winds come to me from the fields of sleep,
    And all the earth is gay;
      Land and sea
  Give themselves up to jollity,
  And with the heart of May
  Doth every beast keep holiday;—
    Thou child of joy,
Shout round me, let me hear thy shouts, thou happy
    Shepherd-boy!

Ye blessèd Creatures, I have heard the call
  Ye to each other make; I see
The heavens laugh with you in your jubilee;
  My heart is at your festival,
  My head hath its coronal,
The fullness of your bliss, I feel—I feel it all.
  O evil day! if I were sullen
  While Earth herself is adorning
    This sweet May-morning;
  And the children are culling
    On every side
  In a thousand valleys far and wide
  Fresh flowers; while the sun shines warm,
And the babe leaps up on his mother's arm:—
  I hear, I hear, with joy I hear!

—But there's a tree, of many, one,
A single field which I have looked upon,
Both of them speak of something that is gone:
    The pansy at my feet
    Doth the same tale repeat:
Whither is fled the visionary gleam?
Where is it now, the glory and the dream?

Our birth is but a sleep and a forgetting;
The Soul that rises with us, our life's Star,
    Hath had elsewhere its setting
        And cometh from afar;
    Not in entire forgetfulness,
    And not in utter nakedness,
But trailing clouds of glory do we come
    From God, who is our home:
Heaven lies about us in our infancy!
Shades of the prison-house begin to close
    Upon the growing Boy,
But he beholds the light, and whence it flows,
    He sees it in his joy;
The Youth, who daily farther from the east
    Must travel, still is Nature's priest,
        And by the vision splendid
        Is on his way attended;
At length the Man perceives it die away,
And fade into the light of common day.

Earth fills her lap with pleasures of her own;
Yearnings she hath in her own natural kind;
And, even with something of a mother's mind,
    And no unworthy aim,
  The homely nurse doth all she can
To make her foster-child, her inmate, Man,
    Forget the glories he hath known,
And that imperial palace whence he came.

Behold the Child among his new-born blisses,
A six years' darling of a pigmy size!
See, where 'mid work of his own hand he lies,
Fretted by sallies of his mother's kisses,
With light upon him from his father's eyes!
See, at his feet, some little plan or chart,
Some fragment from his dream of human life,
Shaped by himself with newly-learned art;
    A wedding or a festival,
    A mourning or a funeral;
        And this hath now his heart,
    And unto this he frames his song:
    Then will he fit his tongue
To dialogues of business, love, or strife;
    But it will not be long
    Ere this be thrown aside,
    And with new joy and pride
The little actor cons another part;
Filling from time to time his 'humorous stage'

With all the Persons, down to palsied Age,
That life brings with her in her equipage;
    As if his whole vocation
    Were endless imitation.

Thou, whose exterior semblance doth belie
    Thy soul's immensity;
Thou best philosopher, who yet dost keep
Thy heritage, thou eye among the blind,
That, deaf and silent, read'st the eternal deep,
Haunted for ever by the eternal Mind,—
    Mighty Prophet! Seer blest!
    On whom those truths rest
Which we are toiling all our lives to find,
In darkness lost, the darkness of the grave;
Thou, over whom thy Immortality
Broods like the day, a master o'er a slave,
A Presence which is not to be put by;
    To whom the grave
Is but a lonely bed, without the sense or sight
    Of day or the warm light,
A place of thought where we in waiting lie;
Thou little child, yet glorious in the might
Of heaven-born freedom on thy being's height,
Why with such earnest pains dost thou provoke
The years to bring the inevitable yoke,
Thus blindly with thy blessedness at strife?
Full soon thy soul shall have her earthly freight,

And custom lie upon thee with a weight
Heavy as frost, and deep almost as life!

    O joy! that in our embers
    Is something that doth live,
    That Nature yet remembers
    What was so fugitive!
The thought of our past years in me doth breed
Perpetual benediction: not indeed
For that which is most worthy to be blest,
Delight and liberty, the simple creed
Of childhood, whether busy or at rest,
With new-fledged hope still fluttering in his breast:—
    —Not for these I raise
    The song of thanks and praise;
But for those obstinate questionings
    Of sense and outward things,
    Fallings from us, vanishings,
    Blank misgivings of a Creature
Moving about in worlds not realised,
High instincts, before which our mortal nature
Did tremble like a guilty thing surprised:
    But for those first affections,
    Those shadowy recollections,
      Which, be they what they may,
Are yet the fountain-light of all our day,
Are yet a master-light of all our seeing;
    Uphold us—cherish—and have power to make

Our noisy years seem moments in the being
Of the eternal Silence: truths that wake,
        To perish never;
Which neither listlessness, nor mad endeavour,
        Nor Man nor Boy,
Nor all that is at enmity with joy,
Can utterly abolish or destroy!
    Hence, in a season of calm weather
        Though inland far we be,
Our souls have sight of that immortal sea
        Which brought us hither;
    Can in a moment travel thither—
And see the children sport upon the shore,
And hear the mighty waters rolling evermore.

Then, sing, ye birds, sing, sing a joyous song!
    And let the young lambs bound
    As to the tabor's sound!
We, in thought, will join your throng,
    Ye that pipe and ye that play,
    Ye that through your hearts to-day
    Feel the gladness of the May!
What though the radiance which was once so bright
Be now for ever taken from my sight,
    Though nothing can bring back the hour
Of splendour in the grass, of glory in the flower;
    We will grieve not, rather find
    Strength in what remains behind;

In the primal sympathy
Which having been must ever be;
In the soothing thoughts that spring
Out of human suffering;
In the faith that looks through death,
In years that bring the philosophic mind.

And o, ye Fountains, Meadows, Hills, and Groves,
Forebode not any severing of our loves!
Yet in my heart of hearts I feel your might;
I only have relinquished one delight
To live beneath your more habitual sway;
I love the brooks which down their channels fret
Even more than when I tripped lightly as they;
The innocent brightness of a new-born day
     Is lovely yet;
The clouds that gather round the setting sun
Do take a sober colouring from an eye
That hath kept watch o'er man's mortality;
Another race hath been, and other palms are won.
Thanks to the human heart by which we live,
Thanks to its tenderness, its joys, and fears,
To me the meanest flower that blows can give
Thoughts that do often lie too deep for tears.

Growth of Man

Emily Dickinson

Growth of Man—like Growth of Nature—
Gravitates within—
Atmosphere, and Sun endorse it
Bit it stir—alone—

Each—its difficult Ideal
Must achieve—Itself—
Through the solitary prowess
Of a Silent Life—

Effort—is the sole condition—
Patience of Itself—
Patience of opposing forces—
And intact Belief—

Looking on—is the Department
Of its Audience—
But Transaction—is assisted
By no Countenance—

Ruins of a Great House

Derek Walcott

though our longest sun sets at right declensions and
makes but winter arches,
it cannot be long before we lie down in darkness, and
have our light in ashes . . .

Browne: Urn Burial

Stones only, the disjecta membra of this Great House,
Whose moth-like girls are mixed with candledust,
Remain to file the lizard's dragonish claws.
The mouths of those gate cherubs shriek with stain;
Axle and coach wheel silted under the muck
Of cattle droppings.
Three crows flap for the trees
And settle, creaking the eucalyptus boughs.
A smell of dead limes quickens in the nose
The leprosy of empire.
'Farewell, green fields,
Farewell, ye happy groves!'

Marble like Greece, like Faulkner's South in stone,
Deciduous beauty prospered and is gone,
But where the lawn breaks in a rash of trees
A spade below dead leaves will ring the bone
Of some dead animal or human thing
Fallen from evil days, from evil times.

It seems that the original crops were limes
Grown in the silt that clogs the river's skirt;

The imperious rakes are gone, their bright girls gone,
The river flows, obliterating hurt.
I climbed a wall with the grille ironwork
Of exiled craftsmen protecting that great house
From guilt, perhaps, but not from the worm's rent
Nor from the padded cavalry of the mouse.
And when a wind shook in the limes I heard
What Kipling heard, the death of a great empire, the abuse
Of ignorance by Bible and by sword.

A green lawn, broken by low walls of stone,
Dipped to the rivulet, and pacing, I thought next
Of men like Hawkins, Walter Raleigh, Drake,
Ancestral murderers and poets, more perplexed
In memory now by every ulcerous crime.
The world's green age then was a rotting lime
Whose stench became the charnel galleon's text.
The rot remains with us, the men are gone.
But, as dead ash is lifted in a wind
That fans the blackening ember of the mind,
My eyes burned from the ashen prose of Donne.

Ablaze with rage I thought,
Some slave is rotting in this manorial lake,
But still the coal of my compassion fought
That Albion too was once
A colony like ours, 'part of the continent, piece of the main',
Nook-shotten, rook o'erblown, deranged

By foaming channels and the vain expense
Of bitter faction.
All in compassion ends
So differently from what the heart arranged:
'as well as if a manor of thy friend's . . .'

From The Rubáiyát

Omar Khayyám

16

Think, in this batter'd Caravanserai
Whose Doorways are alternate Night and Day,
How Sultán after Sultán with his Pomp
Abode his Hour or two, and went his way.

17

They say the Lion and the Lizard keep
The Courts where Jamshýd gloried and drank deep;
And Bahrám, that great Hunter—the Wild Ass
Stamps o'er his Head, and he lies fast asleep.

18

I sometimes think that never blows so red
The Rose as where some buried Caesar bled;
That every Hyacinth the Garden wears
Dropt in its Lap from some once lovely Head.

19

And this delightful Herb whose tender Green
Fledges the River's Lip on which we lean—
Ah, lean upon it lightly! for who knows
From what once lovely Lip it springs unseen!

20

Oh, my Belovéd, fill the Cup that clears
TO-DAY of past Regrets and future Fears—
To-morrow?—Why, To-morrow I may be
Myself with Yesterday's Sev'n Thousand Years.

Prometheus

Johann Goethe

Cover thy spacious heavens, Zeus,
With clouds of mist,
And, like the boy who lops
The thistles' heads,
Disport with oaks and mountain-peaks,
Yet thou must leave
My earth still standing;
My cottage too, which was not raised by thee;
Leave me my hearth,
Whose kindly glow
By thee is envied.

I know nought poorer
Under the sun, than ye gods!
Ye nourish painfully,
With sacrifices
And votive prayers,
Your majesty:
Ye would e'en starve,
If children and beggars
Were not trusting fools.

While yet a child
And ignorant of life,
I turned my wandering gaze
Up tow'rd the sun, as if with him
There were an ear to hear my wailings,

A heart, like mine,
To feel compassion for distress.

Who help'd me
Against the Titans' insolence?
Who rescued me from certain death,
From slavery?
Didst thou not do all this thyself,
My sacred glowing heart?
And glowedst, young and good,
Deceived with grateful thanks
To yonder slumbering one?

I honour thee! and why?
Hast thou e'er lighten'd the sorrows
Of the heavy laden?
Hast thou e'er dried up the tears
Of the anguish-stricken?
Was I not fashion'd to be a man
By omnipotent Time,
And by eternal Fate,
Masters of me and thee?

Didst thou e'er fancy
That life I should learn to hate,
And fly to deserts,
Because not all
My blossoming dreams grew ripe?

Here sit I, forming mortals
After my image;
A race resembling me,
To suffer, to weep,
To enjoy, to be glad,
And thee to scorn,
As I!

In the Dark Times

For Walter Benjamin

Bertolt Brecht

In the dark times
Will there also be singing?
Yes, there will also be singing.
About the dark times.

How can you bear to look at the Neva?

Anna Akhmatova

How can you bear to look at the Neva?
How can you bear to cross the bridges?
Not in vain am I known as the grieving one
Since the time you appeared to me.
The black angels' wings are sharp,
Judgement Day is coming soon,
And raspberry-coloured bonfires bloom,
Like roses, in the snow.

But wise men perceive approaching things

C.P. Cavafy

Because gods perceive future things, men what is happening now,
but wise men perceive approaching things.
> Philostratus, *Life of Apollonius of Tyana, VIII, 7*

Men know what is happening now.
The gods know the things of the future,
the full and sole possessors of all lights.
Of the future things, wise men perceive
approaching things. Their hearing

is sometimes, during serious studies,
disturbed. The mystical clamour
of approaching events reaches them.
And they heed it with reverence. While outside
on the street, the peoples hear nothing at all.

The Famous Victory of Saarbrucken

Arthur Rimbaud

At centre, the Emperor, blue-yellow, in apotheosis,
Gallops off, ramrod straight, on his fine gee-gee,
Very happy—since everything he sees is rosy,
Fierce as Zeus, and as gentle as a Daddy is:

The brave Infantrymen taking a nap, in vain,
Under the gilded drums and scarlet cannon,
Rise politely. One puts his tunic back on,
And turns to the Chief, stunned by the big name!

On the right, another, leaning on his rifle butt,
Feeling the hair rise at the back of his neck,
Shouts: 'Vive L'Empereur!!'—his neighbour's mute . . .

A shako rises, like a black sun . . . —In the midst
The last, a simpleton in red and blue, lying on his gut
Gets up, and,—showing his arse—asks: 'On what?'

The Gods of the Copybook Headings

Rudyard Kipling

As I pass through my incarnations in every age and race,
I make my proper prostrations to the Gods of the Market Place.
Peering through reverent fingers I watch them flourish and fall,
And the Gods of the Copybook Headings, I notice, outlast them all.

We were living in trees when they met us. They showed us each in turn
That Water would certainly wet us, as Fire would certainly burn:
But we found them lacking in Uplift, Vision and Breadth of Mind,
So we left them to teach the Gorillas while we followed the March
   of Mankind.

We moved as the Spirit listed. They never altered their pace,
Being neither cloud nor wind-borne like the Gods of the Market Place,
But they always caught up with our progress, and presently word
   would come
That a tribe had been wiped off its icefield, or the lights had gone
   out in Rome.

With the Hopes that our World is built on they were utterly out of touch,
They denied that the Moon was Stilton; they denied she was even Dutch;
They denied that Wishes were Horses; they denied that a Pig had Wings;
So we worshipped the Gods of the Market Who promised these
   beautiful things.

When the Cambrian measures were forming, They promised
   perpetual peace.
They swore, if we gave them our weapons, that the wars of the tribes
   would cease.

But when we disarmed They sold us and delivered us bound to our
 foe,
And the Gods of the Copybook Headings said: '*Stick to the Devil
 you know.*'

On the first Feminian Sandstones we were promised the Fuller Life
(Which started by loving our neighbour and ended by loving his wife)
Till our women had no more children and the men lost reason and
 faith,
And the Gods of the Copybook Headings said: '*The Wages of Sin is Death.*'

In the Carboniferous Epoch we were promised abundance for all,
By robbing selected Peter to pay for collective Paul;
But, though we had plenty of money, there was nothing our money
 could buy,
And the Gods of the Copybook Headings said: '*If you don't work
 you die.*'

Then the Gods of the Market tumbled, and their smooth-tongued
 wizards withdrew
And the hearts of the meanest were humbled and began to believe
 it was true
That All is not Gold that Glitters, and Two and Two make Four
And the Gods of the Copybook Headings limped up to explain it
 once more.

As it will be in the future, it was at the birth of Man
There are only four things certain since Social Progress began.

That the Dog returns to his Vomit and the Sow returns to her Mire,
And the burnt Fool's bandaged finger goes wabbling back to the Fire;

And that after this is accomplished, and the brave new world begins
When all men are paid for existing and no man must pay for his
    sins,
As surely as Water will wet us, as surely as Fire will burn,
The Gods of the Copybook Headings with terror and slaughter
    return!

All of You Undisturbed Cities

Rainer Maria Rilke

All of you undisturbed cities,
haven't you ever longed for the Enemy?
I'd like to see you besieged by him
for ten endless and ground-shaking years.

Until you were desperate and mad with suffering;
finally in hunger you would feel his weight.
He lies outside the walls like a countryside.
And he knows very well how to endure
longer than the ones he comes to visit.

Climb up on your roofs and look out:
his camp is there and his morale doesn't falter,
and his numbers do not decrease;
he will not grow weaker,
and he sends no one into the city
to threaten or promise,
and no one to negotiate.

He is the one who breaks down the walls,
and when he works, he works in silence.

Hugh Selwyn Mauberley (Part I)

(Life and Contacts)

'Vocat aestus in umbram'

Nemesianus Ec. IV.

E. P. ODE POUR L'ÉLECTION DE SON SÉPULCHRE

Ezra Pound

For three years, out of key with his time,
He strove to resuscitate the dead art
Of poetry; to maintain 'the sublime'
In the old sense. Wrong from the start—

No, hardly, but, seeing he had been born
In a half savage country, out of date;
Bent resolutely on wringing lilies from the acorn;
Capaneus; trout for factitious bait:

'Idmen gar toi panth, os eni Troie
Caught in the unstopped ear;
Giving the rocks small lee-way
The chopped seas held him, therefore, that year.

His true Penelope was Flaubert,
He fished by obstinate isles;
Observed the elegance of Circe's hair
Rather than the mottoes on sun-dials.

Unaffected by 'the march of events',
He passed from men's memory in *l'an trentuniesme*

De son eage; the case presents
No adjunct to the Muses' diadem.

II
The age demanded an image
Of its accelerated grimace,
Something for the modern stage,
Not, at any rate, an Attic grace;

Not, not certainly, the obscure reveries
Of the inward gaze;
Better mendacities
Than the classics in paraphrase!

The 'age demanded' chiefly a mould in plaster,
Made with no loss of time,
A prose kinema, not, not assuredly, alabaster
Or the 'sculpture' of rhyme.

III
The tea-rose, tea-gown, etc.
Supplants the mousseline of Cos,
The pianola 'replaces'
Sappho's barbitos.

Christ follows Dionysus,
Phallic and ambrosial

Made way for macerations;
Caliban casts out Ariel.

All things are a flowing,
Sage Heracleitus says;
But a tawdry cheapness
Shall reign throughout our days.

Even the Christian beauty
Defects—after Samothrace;
We see *to kalon*
Decreed in the market place.

Faun's flesh is not to us,
Nor the saint's vision.
We have the press for wafer;
Franchise for circumcision.

All men, in law, are equals.
Free of Peisistratus,
We choose a knave or an eunuch
To rule over us.

A bright Apollo,

tin andra, tin eroa, tina theon,
What god, man, or hero
Shall I place a tin wreath upon?

IV

These fought, in any case,
and some believing, pro domo, in any case . . .

Some quick to arm,
some for adventure,
some from fear of weakness,
some from fear of censure,
some for love of slaughter, in imagination,
learning later . . .

some in fear, learning love of slaughter;
Died some pro patria, non dulce non et decor' . . .

walked eye-deep in hell
believing in old men's lies, then unbelieving
came home, home to a lie,
home to many deceits,
home to old lies and new infamy;

usury age-old and age-thick
and liars in public places.

Daring as never before, wastage as never before.
Young blood and high blood,
Fair cheeks, and fine bodies;

fortitude as never before

frankness as never before,
disillusions as never told in the old days,
hysterias, trench confessions,
laughter out of dead bellies.

V

There died a myriad,
And of the best, among them,
For an old bitch gone in the teeth,
For a botched civilisation.

Charm, smiling at the good mouth,
Quick eyes gone under earth's lid,

For two gross of broken statues,
For a few thousand battered books.

YEUX GLAUQUES

Gladstone was still respected,
When John Ruskin produced
'Kings Treasuries'; Swinburne
And Rossetti still abused.

Foetid Buchanan lifted up his voice
When that faun's head of hers

Became a pastime for
Painters and adulterers.

The Burne-Jones cartons
Have preserved her eyes;
Still, at the Tate, they teach
Cophetua to rhapsodise;

Thin like brook-water,
With a vacant gaze.
The English Rubaiyat was still-born
In those days.

The thin, clear gaze, the same
Still darts out faun-like from the half-ruin'd face,
Questing and passive . . .
'Ah, poor Jenny's case' . . .
Bewildered that a world
Shows no surprise
At her last maquero's
Adulteries.

'SIENA MI FE', DISFECEMI MAREMMA'

Among the pickled foetuses and bottled bones,
Engaged in perfecting the catalogue,

I found the last scion of the
Senatorial families of Strasbourg, Monsieur Verog.

For two hours he talked of Gallifet;
Of Dowson; of the Rhymers' Club;
Told me how Johnson (Lionel) died
By falling from a high stool in a pub . . .

But showed no trace of alcohol
At the autopsy, privately performed—
Tissue preserved—the pure mind
Arose toward Newman as the whisky warmed.

Dowson found harlots cheaper than hotels;
Headlam for uplift; Image impartially imbued
With raptures for Bacchus, Terpsichore and the Church.
So spoke the author of 'The Dorian Mood',

M. Verog, out of step with the decade,
Detached from his contemporaries,
Neglected by the young,
Because of these reveries.

BRENNBAUM

The sky-like limpid eyes,
The circular infant's face,

The stiffness from spats to collar
Never relaxing into grace;

The heavy memories of Horeb, Sinai and the forty years,
Showed only when the daylight fell
Level across the face
Of Brennbaum 'The Impeccable'.

MR NIXON

In the cream gilded cabin of his steam yacht
Mr Nixon advised me kindly, to advance with fewer
Dangers of delay. 'Consider
   'Carefully the reviewer.

'I was as poor as you are;
'When I began I got, of course,
'Advance on royalties, fifty at first,' said Mr Nixon,
'Follow me, and take a column,
'Even if you have to work free.

'Butter reviewers. From fifty to three hundred
'I rose in eighteen months;
'The hardest nut I had to crack
'Was Dr Dundas.

'I never mentioned a man but with the view
'Of selling my own works.
'The tip's a good one, as for literature
'It gives no man a sinecure.'

And no one knows, at sight a masterpiece.
And give up verse, my boy,
There's nothing in it.'

                    *   *   *   *

Likewise a friend of Bloughram's once advised me:
Don't kick against the pricks,
Accept opinion. The 'Nineties' tried your game
And died, there's nothing in it.

X
Beneath the sagging roof
The stylist has taken shelter,
Unpaid, uncelebrated,
At last from the world's welter

Nature receives him,
With a placid and uneducated mistress
He exercises his talents
And the soil meets his distress.

The haven from sophistications and contentions
Leaks through its thatch;

He offers succulent cooking;
The door has a creaking latch.

XI
'Conservatrix of Milésien'
Habits of mind and feeling,
Possibly. But in Ealing
With the most bank-clerkly of Englishmen?

No, 'Milésien' is an exaggeration.
No instinct has survived in her
Older than those her grandmother
Told her would fit her station.

XII
'Daphne with her thighs in bark
Stretches toward me her leafy hands,'—
Subjectively. In the stuffed-satin drawing-room
I await The Lady Valentine's commands,

Knowing my coat has never been
Of precisely the fashion
To stimulate, in her,
A durable passion;

Doubtful, somewhat, of the value
Of well-gowned approbation

Of literary effort,
But never of The Lady Valentine's vocation:

Poetry, her border of ideas,
The edge, uncertain, but a means of blending
With other strata
Where the lower and higher have ending;

A hook to catch the Lady Jane's attention,
A modulation toward the theatre,
Also, in the case of revolution,
A possible friend and comforter.

*   *   *   *

Conduct, on the other hand, the soul
'Which the highest cultures have nourished'
To Fleet St where
Dr Johnson flourished;

Beside this thoroughfare
The sale of half-hose has
Long since superseded the cultivation
Of Pierian roses.

Envoi (1919)
Go, dumb-born book,
Tell her that sang me once that song of Lawes:

Hadst thou but song
As thou hast subjects known,
Then were there cause in thee that should condone
Even my faults that heavy upon me lie
And build her glories their longevity.

Tell her that sheds
Such treasure in the air,
Recking naught else but that her graces give
Life to the moment,
I would bid them live
As roses might, in magic amber laid,
Red overwrought with orange and all made
One substance and one colour
Braving time.

Tell her that goes
With song upon her lips
But sings not out the song, nor knows
The maker of it, some other mouth,
May be as fair as hers,
Might, in new ages, gain her worshippers,
When our two dusts with Waller's shall be laid,
Siftings on siftings in oblivion,
Till change hath broken down
All things save Beauty alone.

Hawk Roosting

Ted Hughes

I sit in the top of the wood, my eyes closed.
Inaction, no falsifying dream
Between my hooked head and hooked feet:
Or in sleep rehearse perfect kills and eat.

The convenience of the high trees!
The air's buoyancy and the sun's ray
Are of advantage to me;
And the earth's face upward for my inspection.

My feet are locked upon the rough bark.
It took the whole of Creation
To produce my foot, my each feather:
Now I hold Creation in my foot

Or fly up, and revolve it all slowly—
I kill where I please because it is all mine.
There is no sophistry in my body:
My manners are tearing off heads—

The allotment of death.
For the one path of my flight is direct
Through the bones of the living.
No arguments assert my right:

The sun is behind me.
Nothing has changed since I began.

My eye has permitted no change.
I am going to keep things like this.

Inversnaid

Gerard Manley Hopkins

This darksome burn, horseback brown,
His rollrock highroad roaring down,
In coop and in comb the fleece of his foam
Flutes and low to the lake falls home.

A windpuff-bonnet of fáwn-fróth
Turns and twindles over the broth
Of a pool so pitchblack, féll-frówning,
It rounds and rounds Despair to drowning.

Degged with dew, dappled with dew
Are the groins of the braes that the brook treads through,
Wiry heathpacks, flitches of fern,
And the beadbonny ash that sits over the burn.

What would the world be, once bereft
Of wet and of wildness? Let them be left,
O let them be left, wildness and wet;
Long live the weeds and the wilderness yet.

Speech to the Young:
Speech to the Progress-Toward

Gwendolyn Brooks

Say to them,
say to the down-keepers,
the sun-slappers,
the self-soilers,
the harmony-hushers,
'Even if you are not ready for day
it cannot always be night.'
You will be right.
For that is the hard home-run.
Live not for battles won.
Live not for the-end-of-the-song.
Live in the along.

The Second Coming

W.B. Yeats

Turning and turning in the widening gyre
The falcon cannot hear the falconer;
Things fall apart; the centre cannot hold;
Mere anarchy is loosed upon the world,
The blood-dimmed tide is loosed, and everywhere
The ceremony of innocence is drowned;
The best lack all conviction, while the worst
Are full of passionate intensity.

Surely some revelation is at hand;
Surely the Second Coming is at hand.
The Second Coming! Hardly are those words out
When a vast image out of Spiritus Mundi
Troubles my sight: somewhere in sands of the desert
A shape with lion body and the head of a man,
A gaze blank and pitiless as the sun,
Is moving its slow thighs, while all about it
Reel shadows of the indignant desert birds.
The darkness drops again; but now I know
That twenty centuries of stony sleep
Were vexed to nightmare by a rocking cradle,
And what rough beast, its hour come round at last,
Slouches towards Bethlehem to be born?

Isles of Greece

Lord Byron

The isles of Greece, the isles of Greece!
Where burning Sappho loved and sung,
Where grew the arts of war and peace,
Where Delos rose, and Phoebus sprung!
Eternal summer gilds them yet,
But all, except their sun, is set.

The mountains look on Marathon—
And Marathon looks on the sea;
And musing there an hour alone,
I dreamed that Greece might still be free;
For standing on the Persians' grave,
I could not deem myself a slave.

A king sat on the rocky brow
Which looks o'er sea-born Salamis;
And ships, by thousands, lay below,
And men in nations—all were his!
He counted them at break of day—
And when the sun set, where were they?

And where are they? And where art thou?
My country? On thy voiceless shore
The heroic lay is tuneless now—
The heroic bosom beats no more!
And must thy lyre, so long divine,
Degenerate into hands like mine?

'Tis something, in the dearth of fame,
Though linked among a fettered race,
To feel at least a patriot's shame,
Even as I sing, suffuse my face;
For what is left the poet here?
For Greeks a blush—for Greece a tear.

Fill high the bowl with Samian wine!
Our virgins dance beneath the shade—
I see their glorious black eyes shine;
But gazing on each glowing maid,
My own the burning teardrop laves,
To think such breasts must suckle slaves.

Place me on Sunium's marbled steep,
Where nothing, save the waves and I,
May hear our mutual murmurs sweep;
There, swanlike, let me sing and die:
A land of slaves shall ne'er be mine—
Dash down yon cup of Samian wine!

Sonnet LXVI

William Shakespeare

Tir'd with all these, for restful death I cry,
As, to behold desert a beggar born,
And needy nothing trimm'd in jollity,
And purest faith unhappily forsworn,
And guilded honour shamefully misplaced,
And maiden virtue rudely strumpeted,
And right perfection wrongfully disgraced,
And strength by limping sway disabled,
And art made tongue-tied by authority,
And folly (doctor-like) controlling skill,
And simple truth miscall'd simplicity,
And captive good attending captain ill:
  Tired with all these, from these would I be gone,
  Save that, to die, I leave my love alone.

Still I Rise

Maya Angelou

You may write me down in history
With your bitter, twisted lies,
You may trod me in the very dirt
But still, like dust, I'll rise.

Does my sassiness upset you?
Why are you beset with gloom?
'Cause I walk like I've got oil wells
Pumping in my living room.

Just like moons and like suns,
With the certainty of tides,
Just like hopes springing high,
Still I'll rise.

Did you want to see me broken?
Bowed head and lowered eyes?
Shoulders falling down like teardrops,
Weakened by my soulful cries?

Does my haughtiness offend you?
Don't you take it awful hard
'Cause I laugh like I've got gold mines
Diggin' in my own backyard.

You may shoot me with your words,
You may cut me with your eyes,

You may kill me with your hatefulness,
But still, like air, I'll rise.

Does my sexiness upset you?
Does it come as a surprise
That I dance like I've got diamonds
At the meeting of my thighs?

Out of the huts of history's shame
I rise
Up from a past that's rooted in pain
I rise
I'm a black ocean, leaping and wide,
Welling and swelling I bear in the tide.

Leaving behind nights of terror and fear
I rise
Into a daybreak that's wondrously clear
I rise
Bringing the gifts that my ancestors gave,
I am the dream and the hope of the slave.
I rise
I rise
I rise.

Your Logic Frightens Me, Mandela

Wole Soyinka

Your logic frightens me, Mandela
Your logic frightens me. Those years
Of dreams, of time accelerated in
Visionary hopes, of savouring the task anew,
The call, the tempo primed
To burst in supernovae round a 'brave new world'!
Then stillness. Silence. The world closes round
Your sole reality; the rest is . . . dreams?

Your logic frightens me.
How coldly you disdain legerdemains!
'Open Sesame' and—two decades' rust on hinges
Peels at the touch of a conjurer's wand?
White magic, ivory-topped black magic wand,
One moment wand, one moment riot club
Electric cattle prod and whip or sjambok

This bag of tricks, whose silk streamers
Turn knotted cords to crush dark temples?
A rabbit punch sneaked beneath the rabbit?
Doves metamorphosed in milk-white talons?
Not for you the olive branch that sprouts
Gun muzzles, barbed-wire garlands, tangled thorns
To wreathe the brows of black, unwilling Christs.

Your patience grows inhuman, Mandela.
Do you grow food? Do you make friends
Of mice and lizards? Measure the growth of grass
For time's unhurried pace?

Are you now the crossword puzzle expert?
Chess? Ah, no! Subversion lurks among
Chess pieces. Structured clash of black and white,
Equal ranged and paced? An equal board? No!
Not on Robben Island. Checkers? Bad to worse.
That game has no respect for class or king-serf
Ordered universe. So, Scrabble?

Monopoly? Now, that . . .! You know
The game's modalities, so do they.
Come collection time, the cards read 'White Only'
In the Community Chest. Like a gambler's coin
Both sides heads or tails, the 'Chance' cards read:
Go to jail. Go straight to jail. Do not pass 'GO'.
Do not collect a hundredth rand. Fishes feast,
I think, on those who sought to by-pass 'GO'
On Robben Island.

Your logic frightens me, Mandela, your logic
Humbles me. Do you tame geckos?
Do grasshoppers break your silences?
Bats' radar pips pinpoint your statuesque
Gaze transcending distances at will?
Do moths break wing
Against a light bulb's fitful glow

That brings no searing illumination?
Your sight shifts from moth to bulb,

Rests on its pulse-glow fluctuations—
Are kin feelings roused by a broken arc
Of tungsten trapped in vacuum?

Your pulse, I know, has slowed with earth's
Phlegmatic turns. I know your blood
Sagely warms and cools with seasons,
Responds to the lightest breeze
Yet scorns to race with winds (or hurricanes)
That threaten change on tortoise pads.

Is our world light-years away, Mandela?
Lost in visions of that dare supreme
Against a dire supremacy of race?
What brings you back to earth? The night guard's
Inhuman tramp? A sodden eye transgressing through
The Judas hole. Tell me Mandela,
That guard, is he your prisoner?

Your bounty threatens me, Mandela, that taut
Drumskin of your heart on which our millions
Dance. I fear we latch, fat leeches
On your veins. Our daily imprecisions
Dull keen edges of your will.
Compromises deplete your act's repletion—
Feeding will-voided stomachs of a continent,
What will be left of you, Mandela?

The Mask of Anarchy

Percy Bysshe Shelley

As I lay asleep in Italy
There came a voice from over the Sea,
And with great power it forth led me
To walk in the visions of Poesy.

I met Murder on the way—
He had a mask like Castlereagh—
Very smooth he looked, yet grim;
Seven blood-hounds followed him:

All were fat; and well they might
Be in admirable plight,
For one by one, and two by two,
He tossed them human hearts to chew
Which from his wide cloak he drew.

Next came Fraud, and he had on,
Like Lord Eldon, an ermined gown;
His big tears, for he wept well,
Turned to mill-stones as they fell.

And the little children, who
Round his feet played to and fro,
Thinking every tear a gem,
Had their brains knocked out by them.

Clothed with the Bible, as with light,
And the shadows of the night,

Like Sidmouth, next, Hypocrisy
On a crocodile rode by.

And many more Destructions played
In this ghastly masquerade,
All disguised, even to the eyes,
Like Bishops, lawyers, peers, and spies.

Last came Anarchy: he rode
On a white horse, splashed with blood;
He was pale even to the lips,
Like Death in the Apocalypse.

And he wore a kingly crown;
And in his grasp a sceptre shone;
On his brow this mark I saw—
'I AM GOD, AND KING, AND LAW!'

With a pace stately and fast,
Over English land he passed,
Trampling to a mire of blood
The adoring multitude.

And with a mighty troop around
With their trampling shook the ground,
Waving each a bloody sword,
For the service of their Lord.

And with glorious triumph they
Rode through England proud and gay,
Drunk as with intoxication
Of the wine of desolation.

O'er fields and towns, from sea to sea,
Passed the Pageant swift and free,
Tearing up, and trampling down;
Till they came to London town.

And each dweller, panic-stricken,
Felt his heart with terror sicken
Hearing the tempestuous cry
Of the triumph of Anarchy.

For from pomp to meet him came,
Clothed in arms like blood and flame,
The hired murderers, who did sing
'Thou art God, and Law, and King.

'We have waited weak and lone
For thy coming, Mighty One!
Our purses are empty, our swords are cold,
Give us glory, and blood, and gold.'

Lawyers and priests a motley crowd,
To the earth their pale brows bowed;

Like a bad prayer not over loud,
Whispering—'Thou art Law and God.'—

Then all cried with one accord,
'Thou art King, and God, and Lord;
Anarchy, to thee we bow,
Be thy name made holy now!'

And Anarchy, the Skeleton,
Bowed and grinned to every one,
As well as if his education
Had cost ten millions to the nation.

For he knew the Palaces
Of our Kings were rightly his;
His the sceptre, crown, and globe,
And the gold-inwoven robe.

So he sent his slaves before
To seize upon the Bank and Tower,
And was proceeding with intent
To meet his pensioned Parliament

When one fled past, a maniac maid,
And her name was Hope, she said:
But she looked more like Despair,
And she cried out in the air:

'My father Time is weak and grey
With waiting for a better day;
See how idiot-like he stands,
Fumbling with his palsied hands!

'He has had child after child,
And the dust of death is piled
Over every one but me—
Misery, oh, Misery!'

Then she lay down in the street,
Right before the horses feet,
Expecting, with a patient eye,
Murder, Fraud, and Anarchy.

When between her and her foes
A mist, a light, an image rose.
Small at first, and weak, and frail
Like the vapour of a vale:

Till as clouds grow on the blast,
Like tower-crowned giants striding fast,
And glare with lightnings as they fly,
And speak in thunder to the sky.

It grew—a Shape arrayed in mail
Brighter than the viper's scale,

And upborne on wings whose grain
Was as the light of sunny rain.

On its helm, seen far away,
A planet, like the Morning's, lay;
And those plumes its light rained through
Like a shower of crimson dew.

With step as soft as wind it passed
O'er the heads of men—so fast
That they knew the presence there,
And looked,—but all was empty air.

As flowers beneath May's footstep waken,
As stars from Night's loose hair are shaken,
As waves arise when loud winds call,
Thoughts sprung where'er that step did fall.

And the prostrate multitude
Looked—and ankle-deep in blood,
Hope, that maiden most serene,
Was walking with a quiet mien:

And Anarchy, the ghastly birth,
Lay dead earth upon the earth;
The Horse of Death tameless as wind
Fled, and with his hoofs did grind
To dust the murderers thronged behind.

A rushing light of clouds and splendour,
A sense awakening and yet tender
Was heard and felt—and at its close
These words of joy and fear arose

As if their own indignant Earth
Which gave the sons of England birth
Had felt their blood upon her brow,
And shuddering with a mother's throe

Had turned every drop of blood
By which her face had been bedewed
To an accent unwithstood,—
As if her heart cried out aloud:

'Men of England, heirs of Glory,
Heroes of unwritten story,
Nurslings of one mighty Mother,
Hopes of her, and one another;

'Rise like Lions after slumber
In unvanquishable number.
Shake your chains to earth like dew
Which in sleep had fallen on you—
Ye are many—they are few.

'What is Freedom?—ye can tell
That which slavery is, too well—

For its very name has grown
To an echo of your own.

'Tis to work and have such pay
As just keeps life from day to day
In your limbs, as in a cell
For the tyrants' use to dwell,

'So that ye for them are made
Loom, and plough, and sword, and spade,
With or without your own will bent
To their defence and nourishment.

"Tis to see your children weak
With their mothers pine and peak,
When the winter winds are bleak,—
They are dying whilst I speak.

"Tis to hunger for such diet
As the rich man in his riot
Casts to the fat dogs that lie
Surfeiting beneath his eye;

"Tis to let the Ghost of Gold
Take from Toil a thousandfold
More than e'er its substance could
In the tyrannies of old.

'Paper coin—that forgery
Of the title-deeds, which ye
Hold to something from the worth
Of the inheritance of Earth.

''Tis to be a slave in soul
And to hold no strong control
Over your own wills, but be
All that others make of ye.

'And at length when ye complain
With a murmur weak and vain
'Tis to see the Tyrant's crew
Ride over your wives and you—
Blood is on the grass like dew.

'Then it is to feel revenge
Fiercely thirsting to exchange
Blood for blood—and wrong for wrong—
Do not thus when ye are strong.

'Birds find rest, in narrow nest
When weary of their wingèd quest;
Beasts find fare, in woody lair
When storm and snow are in the air.

'Horses, oxen, have a home,
When from daily toil they come;

Household dogs, when the wind roars,
Find a home within warm doors.

'Asses, swine, have litter spread
And with fitting food are fed;
All things have a home but one—
Thou, Oh, Englishman, hast none!

'This is Slavery—savage men,
Or wild beasts within a den
Would endure not as ye do—
But such ills they never knew.

'What art thou, Freedom? O! could slaves
Answer from their living graves
This demand—tyrants would flee
Like a dream's imagery:

'Thou are not, as impostors say,
A shadow soon to pass away,
A superstition, and a name
Echoing from the cave of Fame.

'For the labourer thou art bread,
And a comely table spread
From his daily labour come
In a neat and happy home.

'Thou art clothes, and fire, and food
For the trampled multitude—
No—in countries that are free
Such starvation cannot be
As in England now we see.

'To the rich thou art a check,
When his foot is on the neck
Of his victim, thou dost make
That he treads upon a snake.

'Thou art Justice—ne'er for gold
May thy righteous laws be sold
As laws are in England—thou
Shield'st alike both high and low.

'Thou art Wisdom—Freemen never
Dream that God will damn for ever
All who think those things untrue
Of which Priests make such ado.

'Thou art Peace—never by thee
Would blood and treasure wasted be
As tyrants wasted them, when all
Leagued to quench thy flame in Gaul.

'What if English toil and blood
Was poured forth, even as a flood?

It availed, Oh, Liberty.
To dim, but not extinguish thee.

'Thou art Love—the rich have kissed
Thy feet, and like him following Christ,
Give their substance to the free
And through the rough world follow thee,

'Or turn their wealth to arms, and make
War for thy belovèd sake
On wealth, and war, and fraud—whence they
Drew the power which is their prey.

'Science, Poetry, and Thought
Are thy lamps; they make the lot
Of the dwellers in a cot
So serene, they curse it not.

'Spirit, Patience, Gentleness,
All that can adorn and bless
Art thou—let deeds, not words, express
Thine exceeding loveliness.

'Let a great Assembly be
Of the fearless and the free
On some spot of English ground
Where the plains stretch wide around.

'Let the blue sky overhead,
The green earth on which ye tread,
All that must eternal be
Witness the solemnity.

'From the corners uttermost
Of the bounds of English coast;
From every hut, village, and town
Where those who live and suffer moan
For others' misery or their own,

'From the workhouse and the prison
Where pale as corpses newly risen,
Women, children, young and old
Groan for pain, and weep for cold—

'From the haunts of daily life
Where is waged the daily strife
With common wants and common cares
Which sows the human heart with tares—

'Lastly from the palaces
Where the murmur of distress
Echoes, like the distant sound
Of a wind alive around

'Those prison halls of wealth and fashion,
Where some few feel such compassion

For those who groan, and toil, and wail
As must make their brethren pale—

'Ye who suffer woes untold,
Or to feel, or to behold
Your lost country bought and sold
With a price of blood and gold—

'Let a vast assembly be,
And with great solemnity
Declare with measured words that ye
Are, as God has made ye, free—

'Be your strong and simple words
Keen to wound as sharpened swords,
And wide as targes let them be,
With their shade to cover ye.

'Let the tyrants pour around
With a quick and startling sound,
Like the loosening of a sea,
Troops of armed emblazonry.

'Let the charged artillery drive
Till the dead air seems alive
With the clash of clanging wheels,
And the tramp of horses' heels.

'Let the fixèd bayonet
Gleam with sharp desire to wet
Its bright point in English blood
Looking keen as one for food.

'Let the horsemen's scimitars
Wheel and flash, like sphereless stars
Thirsting to eclipse their burning
In a sea of death and mourning.

'Stand ye calm and resolute,
Like a forest close and mute,
With folded arms and looks which are
Weapons of unvanquished war,

'And let Panic, who outspeeds
The career of armèd steeds
Pass, a disregarded shade
Through your phalanx undismayed.

'Let the laws of your own land,
Good or ill, between ye stand
Hand to hand, and foot to foot,
Arbiters of the dispute,

'The old laws of England—they
Whose reverend heads with age are grey,
Children of a wiser day;

And whose solemn voice must be
Thine own echo—Liberty!

'On those who first should violate
Such sacred heralds in their state
Rest the blood that must ensue,
And it will not rest on you.

'And if then the tyrants dare
Let them ride among you there,
Slash, and stab, and maim, and hew,—
What they like, that let them do.

'With folded arms and steady eyes,
And little fear, and less surprise,
Look upon them as they slay
Till their rage has died away.

'Then they will return with shame
To the place from which they came,
And the blood thus shed will speak
In hot blushes on their cheek.

'Every woman in the land
Will point at them as they stand—
They will hardly dare to greet
Their acquaintance in the street.

'And the bold, true warriors
Who have hugged Danger in wars
Will turn to those who would be free,
Ashamed of such base company.

'And that slaughter to the Nation
Shall steam up like inspiration,
Eloquent, oracular;
A volcano heard afar.

'And these words shall then become
Like Oppression's thundered doom
Ringing through each heart and brain.
Heard again—again—again—

'Rise like Lions after slumber
In unvanquishable number—
Shake your chains to earth like dew
Which in sleep had fallen on you—
Ye are many—they are few.'

Acknowledgements

I would like to thank Rupert Lancaster at Hodder & Stoughton who commissioned this book and Beth Dufour for all her work in clearing the permissions.

Ben Okri and the publishers gratefully acknowledge permission to reprint copyright material in this collection as follows below:

Anna Akhmatova, 'I hear the Oriole's always-grieving voice', 'And you, my Friends who have been Called Away' and 'How can you Bear to Look at the Neva'. Penguin Books Ltd.

Maya Angelou, 'Still I Rise', from *And Still I Rise: A Book Of Poems*. Copyright © 1978 by Maya Angelou. Used by permission of Virago and of Random House, an imprint and division of Penguin Random House LLC. All rights reserved.

W. H. Auden, 'Oh What is that Sound', Copyright © 1940 by W.H. Auden, renewed. Reprinted by permission of Curtis Brown, Ltd.

Matsuo Basho, 'Come, See Real Flowers', 'Don't Forget the Plum' and 'Poet Grieving over Shivering Monkeys'. Penguin Books Ltd.

Bertolt Brecht, 'Motto: In den finsteren Zeiten', 1939 , English translation, 'In the Dark Times' by Thomas Mark Kuhn. Copyright © 1961, 1976 by Bertolt-Brecht-Erben / Suhrkamp Verlag, 'Fragen eines lesenden Arbeiters', 1936 as English transation, 'Questions of a worker who reads' by Thomas Mark Kuhn. Copyright © 1961, 1976 by Bertolt-Brecht-Erben / Suhrkamp Verlag, 'Dass ihr hier sitzen könnt', 1955, English translation, 'So you could sit here...' by Thomas Mark Kuhn. Copyright © 1964, 1976 by Bertolt-Brecht-Erben / Suhrkamp Verlag, 'Solidaritatslied', 1931, English translation, 'Solidarity Song' by David J. Constantine. Copyright © 1961, 1976 by Bertolt-Brecht-Erben / Suhrkamp Verlag, from *Collected Poems of Bertolt Brecht* by Bertolt Brecht, translated by Thomas Mark

Index of titles

Index of poets

Index of first lines